Linux Essentials for Hackers & Pentesters

Kali Linux Basics for Wireless Hacking, Penetration Testing, VPNs, Proxy Servers and Networking Commands

Linux Advocate Team

ISBN: 978-8196228514

Contents

PREFACE

"Linux Essentials for Hackers & Pentesters" is a hands-on tutorial-style book that teaches you the fundamentals of Linux with an emphasis on ethical hacking and penetration testing. This book employs the Kali Linux distribution to teach readers how to use Linux commands and packages to perform security testing on systems and networks.

Text manipulation, network administration, ownership and permissions, BASH scripting, proxy servers, VPNs, and wireless networks are all covered. The book prepares you to perform web application hacking and build your own hacking linux toolkit by teaching you how to use linux commands and beginning to think like a hacker. Hands-on exercises and practical examples are included in each chapter to reinforce the concepts covered.

This book is a must-have for anyone interested in a career in ethical hacking and penetration testing. Emphasizing on ethical hacking practises, you'll learn not only how to hack but also how to do so responsibly and legally. This book will provide you with the skills and knowledge you need to make a positive impact in the field of cybersecurity while also acting ethically and professionally. This book will help you hone your skills and become a skilled and ethical Linux hacker, whether you're a beginner or an experienced hacker.

In this book, you make yourself confident in working around:

- Learning linux binaries, complex text patterns, and combining commands
- Modifying and cloning IP addresses, phishing MAC ID, accessing and troubleshooting DNS
- Manipulating ownership and permissions, exploring sensitive files and writing BASH scripts
- Working around disk partitioning, filesystem errors and logical volume management
- Accessing proxy server policies, intercepting server performance and manipulating proxy servers
- Setting up APs, firewalls, VLAN, managing access, WPA encryption, and network analysis using Wireshark

GitforGits

Prerequisites

If you are just getting started on the exciting path of hacking, cybersecurity, and penetration testing, an excellent first step is to read Linux Essentials for Hackers and Pentesters. This book will teach you the fundamentals of Linux in these fields.

You don't need any prior knowledge of Linux or security concepts to follow along with the instructions in this book, so chill out.

Codes Usage

Are you in need of some helpful code examples to assist you in your programming and documentation? Look no further! Our book offers a wealth of supplemental material, including code examples and exercises.

Not only is this book here to aid you in getting your job done, but you have our permission to use the example code in your programs and documentation. However, please note that if you are reproducing a significant portion of the code, we do require you to contact us for Permission.

But don't worry, using several chunks of code from this book in your program or answering a question by citing our book and quoting example code does not require permission. But if you do choose to give credit, an attribution typically includes the title, author, publisher, and ISBN. For example, "Linux Essentials For Hackers & PenTesters by the Linux Advocate Team".

If you are unsure whether your intended use of the code examples falls under fair use or the permissions outlined above, please do not hesitate to reach out to us at kittenpub.kdp@gmail.com.

We are happy to assist and clarify any concerns.

Acknowledgement

The linux advocate team would express their gratitude to all of the other contributors to linux and work tirelessly to improve the quality of the operating system. While they are doing this, they would want to express their gratitude to the copywriters, tech editors, and reviewers who helped create a powerful yet simple book that outperforms rust coding in a relatively short period of time.

CHAPTER 1: UP AND RUNNING WITH LINUX BASICS

Understanding Terminal

Introduction

The majority of people who use the operating system Kali Linux are professionals in the information technology sector, such as network administrators and security experts. These individuals frequently utilize the terminal, which is a powerful tool, in order to carry out tasks such as testing the security of a network or conducting vulnerability analysis, among other tasks. Students and researchers who are pursuing degrees in computer science and information technology also make use of it.

The terminal in Kali Linux is not only used for professional purposes, but also by hobbyists and enthusiasts who are interested in learning more about operating systems and computer security. This is because the terminal in Kali Linux can be used to perform professional tasks. People who are interested in learning more about the inner workings of a computer and how to use the command-line interface frequently go this route because it is a popular option.

Characteristics of Terminal

The following is a list of features that can be found in Kali Linux's terminal:

- Command-line interface: The terminal is a text-based interface that allows users to enter commands using a keyboard.

- Powerful: The terminal can be used to perform a wide variety of tasks, from the simplest file management to the most complex testing of network security.

- Customizable: Users have the ability to create their own scripts and aliases, as well as choose from a variety of shells and command-line utilities when customizing the terminal. This makes it possible for users to automate a variety of tasks.

- No GUI: The terminal does not have a graphical user interface (GUI), so users must rely on text-based commands to interact with the operating system.

- Versatility: The terminal can be used on any operating system, including Kali Linux, making it a useful tool for those familiar with it.

Steps using Terminal in Kali Linux

After becoming familiar with the fundamental commands, utilizing the terminal in Kali Linux is a very straightforward process. The following is an in-depth walkthrough of how to operate the terminal in its various forms:

- Open the terminal: To open the terminal, click on the terminal icon in the taskbar or search for "terminal" in the start menu.

- Enter a command: To enter a command, simply type it into the terminal and press the enter key. For example, you can use the "ls" command to list the files in the current directory.

- Use options and arguments: Many commands have options and arguments that can be used to modify their behavior. Options are usually specified using a single hyphen followed by a letter, and arguments are specific values that are passed to the command. For example, the "ls" command can be used with the "-l" option to display the files in a long format, and the "-a" option to show hidden files.

- View the manual page: To learn more about a particular command, you can use the "man" command to view the manual page for that command. For example, to view the manual page for the "ls" command, you can enter "man ls".

- Use command-line completion: To save time, you can use the tab key to automatically complete a command or file name that you are typing. For example, if you have a file named "report.txt" in the current directory, you can type "cat rep" and then press the tab key to automatically complete the command as "cat report.txt".

- Use the up and down arrow keys: You can use the up and down arrow keys to navigate through the command history and easily reuse previous commands.

- Use the bash shell: The terminal in Kali Linux uses the bash shell by default, which provides a number of useful features such as command history, command-line completion, and aliases.

Exploring Filesystem

Filesystem Hierarchy Standard (FHS)

The term "filesystem" refers to the method by which documents and other types of data are stored and organized on a computer. Users are able to access and manage their files in a manner that is both logical and organized thanks to this hierarchical structure, which consists of directories (also known as folders) and files.

The "/" symbol denotes the root directory, which is the highest-level directory in the filesystem. The root directory is the starting point for all other directories. All of the other directories and files are arranged in a tree-like fashion directly underneath it. For example, the directory "/home" contains the home directories for all users of the system, and the directory "/etc" contains system-wide configuration files.

The filesystem in Kali Linux is typically structured according to the Filesystem Hierarchy Standard (FHS), which specifies a standard directory tree for Unix-like operating systems and is the basis for the filesystem's organization. The File and Directory System (FHS) makes it possible for users to quickly locate files and directories and ensures compatibility with other applications.

Characteristics of Filesystem

Here are a few advanced aspects of the filesystem in Kali Linux:

- File permissions:are Kali Linux, each file and directory has associated permissions that control who can access and modify it. There are three types of permissions: read (r), write (w), and execute (x). These permissions can be set for the owner of the file, the group owner, and other users.

- Links: Links are a way to create multiple references to a single file or directory. There are two types of links: hard links and symbolic links. Hard links create a new directory entry that points to the same inode as the original file, while symbolic links create a special file that contains the path to the original file.

- Mount points: In Kali Linux, devices such as hard drives and removable media are not automatically mounted when they are connected. Instead, they must be manually mounted to a mount point in the filesystem. A mount point is a directory where the device's filesystem will be accessible.

- File system types: Kali Linux supports a wide range of file system types, including ext2, ext3, ext4, NTFS, and more. Different file system types have different features and capabilities, and may be more suitable for certain types of storage or workloads.

- File system utilities: Kali Linux includes a number of utilities that can be used to manage and maintain the filesystem, such as fsck (file system check) and mke2fs (make ext2 file system). These utilities can be used to check and repair file system errors, create and format file systems, and more.

- File system labels: File system labels are optional names that can be assigned to file systems to help identify them. They can be useful when there are multiple file systems on a single device, or when using removable media.

- File system quotas: File system quotas are used to limit the amount of disk space and/or inodes (files and directories) that a user or group can use on a file system. They can be useful for managing disk usage and preventing a single user or group from using up all of the available space.

- File system encryption: Kali Linux includes support for file system encryption, which allows users to protect their data by encrypting their file systems. File system encryption can be useful for protecting sensitive data, especially on portable devices.

Components of Filesystem

Here are some of the main components of the filesystem in Kali Linux:

Directories: A directory, also known as a folder, is a container for files and other directories. It is used to organize files in a hierarchical structure.

Files: A file is a collection of data that is stored on a computer. Files can contain text, images, audio, video, and other types of data.

Inodes: An inode is a data structure that stores information about a file or directory, such as its permissions, size, and location on the disk. Each file and directory in a file system has an associated inode.

Links: Links are a way to create multiple references to a single file or directory. There are two types of links: hard links and symbolic links.

Mount points: A mount point is a directory where a device's filesystem is mounted and made accessible.

File system types: Different file system types have different features and capabilities, and may be more suitable for certain types of storage or workloads.

Popular Commands In-Use

What are Commands?

The term "command" refers to the instructions that are typed into a command-line interface (CLI) or terminal in order to carry out a particular operation. In the context of Kali Linux, commands are entered into the terminal to execute tasks and perform actions on the operating system.

Typical command structure consists of a command name followed by one or more options and arguments in any order. The name of the command indicates the operation that is to be carried out, while the options and arguments either provide additional information or modify the behavior of the command.

For instance, the "ls" command is used to list the files and directories contained in a directory, and the "-l" option can be used to display the files in a long format. Another example:

Kali Linux provides users with access to hundreds of commands, all of which can be used to carry out a diverse range of activities, including the management of files, the execution of programs, the configuration of the system, and many others.

The Implementation of Commands

In Kali Linux, the use of commands is required to carry out a wide variety of tasks, including the following:

- File management: Commands such as "ls", "cd", "cp", and "mv" can be used to list, change, copy, and move files and directories.
- System administration: Commands such as "sudo", "apt get", and "systemctl" can be used to manage system resources, install and update software, and control system services.
- Networking: Commands such as "ifconfig", "ping", and "traceroute" can be used to configure network interfaces, troubleshoot network connectivity, and trace the route between two hosts.
- Security: Commands such as "nmap", "wireshark", and "aircrack-ng" can be used to scan networks, capture and analyze network traffic, and perform wireless security assessments.
- Text processing: Commands such as "grep", "sed", and "awk" can be used to search, replace, and manipulate text.
- Shell scripting: Commands can be combined into scripts to automate tasks and perform complex operations.
- Process management: Commands such as "ps", "top", and "kill" can be used to display and control running processes.
- Disk management: Commands such as "df", "du", and "fdisk" can be used to display disk usage, estimate file space usage, and partition disks.
- File compression and archiving: Commands such as "gzip", "tar", and "zip" can be used to compress and archive files.
- Text editing: Commands such as "vi", "emacs", and "nano" are text editors that can be used to create and modify text files.
- System information: Commands such as "uname", "cat /proc/cpuinfo", and "free" can be used to display system information such as the kernel version, CPU information, and memory usage.
- Package management: Commands such as "dpkg" and "apt" can be used to install, remove, and manage software packages on the system.

25 Everyday Commands for Use

Following is a list of the 25 most common commands used in Kali Linux, along with a brief description of each:

- ls: List the files and directories in a directory
- cd: Change the current directory
- pwd: Print the current working directory
- mkdir: Create a new directory
- rmdir: Remove an empty directory
- cp: Copy files and directories
- mv: Move or rename files and directories
- rm: Remove files and directories
- touch: Create a new file or update the timestamp of an existing file
- cat: Concatenate and display the contents of files
- less: View the contents of a file one page at a time
- grep: Search for patterns in files
- find: Search for files and directories
- head: Display the first lines of a file
- tail: Display the last lines of a file
- sort: Sort the lines of a file

- uniq: Remove duplicate lines from a file
- wc: Count the number of lines, words, and characters in a file
- cut: Extract columns of data from a file
- paste: Combine the contents of multiple files
- diff: Display the differences between two files
- patch: Apply changes to a file using a patch file
- whoami: Display the current user's username
- who: Display information about logged-in users
- passwd: Change the current user's password

Learning Binaries

What are Binaries in Kali?

The term "binaries" refers to files that can be executed after being compiled from their respective source codes. The /usr/bin directory, which is automatically included in the system PATH, is typically where these files are kept, and you can access it by typing "path" in the command prompt. This enables you to execute any binary file by simply typing its name into the command prompt; you are not required to specify the complete path to the file in order to do so.

For instance, if you want to run the ls command, which is used to list the contents of a directory, all you have to do is type ls at the prompt and press the Enter key. This will execute the command. The ls binary will be automatically located and run by the system after it has been downloaded.

TFollowing is a wide variety of software on offer in the form of binaries in the Kali Linux operating system. These binaries include utilities for system administration, tools for managing networks, and other applications. Binaries such as ls, grep, find, ping, nmap, and apt-get are examples of some of the more common binaries in Kali Linux.

Benefits of Binaries

There are several benefits to using binaries in Linux:

- Ease of installation: Binaries are pre-compiled and ready to run, so they are easy to install and use. This is especially useful for users who are not comfortable with compiling source code from scratch.

- Compatibility: Binaries are compiled specifically for a particular version of a Linux distribution, so they are more likely to be compatible with your system.

- Performance: Binaries are optimized for performance, so they may run faster than the equivalent programs compiled from source code.

- Security: Binaries are typically distributed through official package repositories, which means they have been checked for security vulnerabilities. This can provide an additional level of security compared to compiling programs from source code, which may not have been thoroughly tested.

- Convenience: Most Linux distributions include a package manager that makes it easy to install, update, and remove binaries. This is a convenient way to manage the software on your system.

Overall, binaries are an important and useful aspect of the Linux ecosystem, and they make it easy for users to take advantage of the many tools and utilities available in the Linux world.

How to Use Binaries?

Following are the means of using binaries in everyday's use:

- Installing software: Many Linux software packages are distributed as binaries, which can be easily installed using a package manager like apt or yum. For example, to install the nano text editor on Kali Linux, you could use the following command:

```
apt-get install nano
```

- Running system commands: Many of the tools and utilities that are used to manage and maintain a Linux system are available as binaries. For example, you can use the ls command to list the contents of a directory, the cd command to change directories, and the pwd command to display the current working directory.

- Networking tasks: Kali Linux includes a number of networking tools that are available as binaries, such as ping, traceroute, and nmap. These tools can be used to troubleshoot connectivity issues, scan networks for vulnerabilities, and perform other networking tasks.

- Text processing: There are many utilities available for processing text files in Linux, such as grep, sed, and awk. These tools can be used to search for patterns in text, extract information from text files, and perform other text manipulation tasks.

- System administration: There are a wide variety of system administration tools available in Linux, such as systemctl, journalctl, and lsmod. These tools can be used to manage system services, view log files, and manage kernel modules, respectively.

Functionality of Top 50 Binaries

- bash: the Bourne-Again SHell, a command-line interface for interacting with the operating system

- ls: lists the contents of a directory

- cd: changes the current working directory

- pwd: prints the current working directory

- cat: concatenates and prints files

- rm: removes files or directories

- mkdir: creates a new directory

- touch: creates a new file or updates the timestamp of an existing file

- cp: copies files or directories

- mv: moves or renames files or directories
- less: a program for viewing text files
- head: prints the first few lines of a text file
- tail: prints the last few lines of a text file
- grep: searches for patterns in text
- awk: a programming language for text processing
- sed: a stream editor for text manipulation
- tr: translates or deletes characters in a text stream
- cut: extracts selected fields from a file
- paste: combines lines of files
- sort: sorts the lines of a text file
- uniq: removes duplicate lines from a text file
- wc: counts the number of lines, words, and characters in a file
- tee: reads from standard input and writes to both standard output and a file
- find: searches for files in a directory hierarchy
- which: shows the full path of a command
- whereis: locates a command, source code, or documentation for a program
- whoami: shows the current user's login name
- hostname: shows the system's hostname

- who: shows information about users who are currently logged in
- ping: tests connectivity to a remote host
- netstat: shows network connections, routing tables, and interface statistics
- traceroute: shows the path that packets take to a destination
- telnet: connects to a remote host using the Telnet protocol
- ssh: connects to a remote host using the Secure Shell (SSH) protocol
- scp: securely copies files between hosts
- sftp: securely transfers files between hosts using the SFTP protocol
- rsync: synchronizes files between hosts
- wget: retrieves files from the web using HTTP, HTTPS, or FTP
- curl: retrieves data from the web using a variety of protocols
- tar: creates or extracts files from a tar archive
- gzip: compresses or decompresses files using the Gzip algorithm
- bzip2: compresses or decompresses files using the Bzip2 algorithm
- gunzip: decompresses files that were compressed with Gzip
- bunzip2: decompresses files that were compressed with Bzip2
- zip: compresses or decompresses files in the ZIP format
- unzip: extracts files from a ZIP archive
- chmod: changes the permissions on a file or directory

- chown: changes the owner of a file or directory
- chgrp: changes the group ownership of a file or directory
- df: shows the amount of available disk space on the system

Finding Binaries

The process of searching for binaries in Linux is typically not difficult because the operating system comes pre-loaded with a number of commands and tools that can assist users in locating the binaries they require.

For instance, you can use the which, whereis, and locate commands to pinpoint the location of a particular binary file on your computer. The find command can be used to search for files based on their name or other criteria, and the apropos command can be used to search the man page database for keywords related to a specific command. Both of these commands are available through the find and apropos commands.

In addition, the vast majority of Linux distributions come pre-packaged with a package manager that enables users to locate and install various software packages. The majority of these package managers come equipped with a search function that enables users to locate packages based on their names or keywords.

Searching Binaries

There are several ways you can search for binaries in Linux:

Use the which command: This command will show you the full path to the executable file for a given command. For example, to find the location of the ls command, you can use the following command:

```
which ls
```

Use the whereis command: This command will show you the location of the binary, source code, and documentation files for a given command. For example:

```
whereis ls
```

Use the find command: This command can search for files or directories by name or other criteria. For example, to search for all files named ls in the /usr/bin directory, you can use the following command:

```
find /usr/bin -name ls
```

Use the locate command: This command searches a database of file names, rather than the file system itself. It can be faster than the find command, but the database may not be up to date. To search for a file named ls, you can use the following command:

```
locate ls
```

Use the apropos command: This command searches the man page names and descriptions for a given keyword. For example, to search for all man pages related to the ls command, you can use the following command:

```
apropos ls
```

Overall, it is usually not difficult to find binaries in Linux as long as you know what you are looking for and have a basic understanding of the tools and commands that are available to you.

Creating Files and Directories

Essentials of Files and Directories in Kali Linux

In Kali Linux, as in most operating systems, "files" and "directories" are basic concepts that are used to organize and store data.

A "file" is a single unit of data that is stored on a computer's hard drive or other storage device. A file can contain text, images, audio, or other types of data, and it is usually identified by its name and extension, which indicates the type of data it contains. For example, a file named report.txt is a text file, while a file named picture.jpg is a JPEG image.

A "directory" (also known as a "folder") is a container that is used to organize and store files. Directories can contain other directories as well as files, and they can be nested to create a hierarchical structure. The top-level directory in a Linux system is called the "root" directory, and it is designated with a forward slash (/).

In Kali Linux, you can use the ls command to list the files and directories in a directory, the cd command to change the current working directory, and the mkdir command to create a new directory. You can use the cp command to copy files and the mv command to move or rename files. The rm command can be used to delete files, and the rmdir command can be used to delete empty directories.

Create File

To create a new file in Kali Linux, you can use the touch command followed by the name of the file you want to create. For example, to create a new file called test.txt, you can use the following command:

```
touch test.txt
```

This will create an empty file with the name test.txt in the current working directory. If you want to create a file with some initial content, you can use the echo command to write text to the file. For example:

```
echo "This is a test file" > test.txt
```

Create Directory

To create a new directory in Kali Linux, you can use the mkdir command followed by the name of the directory you want to create. For example, to create a new directory called test, you can use the following command:

```
mkdir test
```

You can also create a hierarchy of directories by using the mkdir command with the -p option. For example, to create a new directory called test/subdir, you can use the following command:

```
mkdir -p test/subdir
```

This will create a new directory called subdir inside a directory called test, and will create the test directory if it does not already exist.

Modifying Files and Directories

To modify a file in Kali Linux, you can use a text editor to open the file and make changes to its contents. Some common text editors in Kali Linux include nano, vi, and emacs.

For example, to open the file test.txt in the nano editor, you can use the following command:

```
nano test.txt
```

This will open the test.txt file in the nano editor, and you can use the arrow keys to navigate to the desired location in the file and make changes. When you are finished, you can press Ctrl+X to exit the editor, and then press Y to save your changes.

To modify the name of a file or directory in Kali Linux, you can use the mv command. For example, to rename the file test.txt to sample.txt, you can use the following command:

```
mv test.txt sample.txt
```

To move a file or directory to a different location, you can use the mv command with the name of the file or directory as the first argument and the destination path as the second argument. For example, to move the file sample.txt to the test directory, you can use the following command:

```
mv sample.txt test/
```

To modify the permissions of a file or directory in Kali Linux, you can use the chmod command. This command allows you to specify the read, write, and execute permissions for the file's owner, group, and other users. For example, to give the owner of the file sample.txt read and write permissions, but not execute permission, you can use the following command:

```
chmod u+rw,g-x,o-x sample.txt
```

Deleting Files

To delete a file in Kali Linux, you can use the rm command followed by the name of the file you want to delete. For example, to delete the file sample.txt, you can use the following command:

```
rm sample.txt
```

To delete a directory, you can use the rm command with the -r option to delete the directory and all of its contents. For example, to delete the test directory and all of its contents, you can use the following command:

```
rm -r test/
```

Be careful when using the rm command, as it permanently removes the specified files or directories, and there is no way to recover them.

If you want to delete a directory that is not empty, you can use the rm command with the -r option and the -f option to force the deletion of the directory and all of its contents. For example:

```
rm -rf test/
```

To delete a file or directory that is write-protected, you can use the rm command with the -f option to force the deletion. For example:

```
rm -f sample.txt
```

Summary

Binaries are executable programs in Linux. They are usually stored in directories like /usr/bin and can be invoked from the command line.

There are several ways to search for binaries in Linux, including the which, whereis, find, and locate commands, as well as package managers like apt and yum.

Files are units of data that are stored on a computer's hard drive or other storage device. They are usually identified by their name and extension, which indicates the type of data they contain.

Directories (also known as folders) are containers that are used to organize and store files. They can be nested to create a hierarchical structure, and the top-level directory in a Linux system is called the "root" directory.

In Kali Linux, you can use the ls, cd, mkdir, cp, and mv commands to manage files and directories, and the rm command to delete files or directories. You can also use text editors like nano, vi, and emacs to modify the contents of files.

The chmod command can be used to modify the permissions of a file or directory, and the find, grep, and awk commands can be used to search for and manipulate files and data. The xargs command can be used to operate on a list of files that are generated by other commands.

Hack#1: Operating Multiple Files

Use wildcards to operate on multiple files at once: You can use wildcard characters like * and ? to operate on multiple files at once in Kali Linux. For example, to delete all .txt files in the current directory, you can use the following command:

```
rm *.txt
```

Hack#2: To Find and Operate On Files

Use the find command to locate and operate on files with specific characteristics: The find command is a powerful tool that can be used to locate and operate on files based on various criteria, such as name, size, modification time, and permissions. For example, to find all files in the /usr/bin directory that are larger than 100MB and delete them, you can use the following command:

```
find /usr/bin -size +100M -delete
```

Hack#3: Search For Text Patterns

Use the grep command to search for text patterns in files: The grep command is a powerful tool for searching for patterns of text in files. You can use it to search for specific words, phrases, or regular expressions in one or more files. For example, to search for the word "error" in all .log files in the /var/log directory, you can use the following command:

```
grep error /var/log/*.log
```

Hack#4: Extract and Manipulate Text Files

Use the awk command to extract and manipulate data from text files: The awk command is a programming language that is designed for text processing. You can use it to extract specific fields of data from text files and perform calculations or other manipulations on the data. For example, to extract the second and fourth fields from a tab-delimited file and calculate the average of those fields, you can use the following command:

```
awk '{ sum += $2 + $4; count++ } END { print sum / count }'
data.txt
```

Hack#5: Work On Multiple Files

Use the xargs command to operate on a list of files: The xargs command is used to build and execute a command line from standard input. It is often used in combination with other commands like find or grep to operate on a list of files that are generated by those commands. For example, to find all .txt files in the current directory and copy them to the /tmp directory, you can use the following command:

```
find . -name "*.txt" | xargs cp -t /tmp
```

Chapter 2: How To Manipulate Text?

Overview of Text-Related Commands

In Kali Linux, there are several text related commands that you can use to view, edit, and manipulate text files. Some common examples include:

- cat: displays the contents of a text file to the terminal
- head: displays the first few lines of a text file
- tail: displays the last few lines of a text file
- less: displays a text file one screen at a time
- more: displays a text file one screen at a time, with a prompt to press a key before displaying the next screen
- nl: displays a text file with line numbers
- tac: displays a text file in reverse order (last line first)
- rev: displays a text file with the lines reversed (but not the characters within the lines)

There are also several text editors that you can use to create and modify text files in Kali Linux, such as nano, vi, and emacs.

In addition to these commands, there are also several tools that you can use to search for patterns of text within files, such as grep and sed. The awk command is a programming language that is specifically designed for text processing, and it can be used to extract and manipulate data from text files.

Viewing, Filtering, Extracting…

There are many tasks and operations that you can perform with text commands in Kali Linux. Some examples include:

Viewing the contents of text files: You can use commands like cat, head, tail, less, and more to display the contents of text files to the terminal. The cat command displays the entire contents of the file, while head and tail display the first or last few lines of the file, respectively. The less and more commands display the file one screen at a time, with a prompt to press a key before displaying the next screen. You can use options like -n to display line numbers, -b to display byte counts, or -s to suppress repeated empty lines.

Searching for patterns of text within files: You can use commands like grep and sed to search for specific words, phrases, or regular expressions within text files. The grep command searches for patterns of text in one or more files and displays the matching lines. You can use options like -i to ignore case, -v to display non-matching lines, or -n to display line numbers. The sed command is a stream editor that can be used to search for and replace patterns of text within a file or stream of data.

Extracting and manipulating data from text files: You can use the awk command to extract specific fields of data from text files and perform calculations or other manipulations on the data. The awk command reads a file or stream of data one line at a time and divides each line into fields based on a delimiter (such as a tab or a space). You can then use patterns and actions to specify what to do with each line of data. For example, you could use awk to extract the second and fourth fields from a tab-delimited file and calculate the average of those fields, like this:

```
awk '{ sum += $2 + $4; count++ } END { print sum / count }'
data.txt
```

Sorting the lines of a text file: You can use the sort command to sort the lines of a text file alphabetically or numerically. The sort command reads a file or stream of data and sorts the lines in ascending order. You can use options like -r to sort in descending order, -n to sort numerically, or -k to specify a field to sort by.

Removing duplicate lines from a text file: You can use the uniq command to remove duplicate lines from a text file, or to count the number of times each line appears in the file. The uniq command reads a file or stream of data and compares adjacent lines to see if they are identical. If a line appears more than once, only the first occurrence is displayed. You can use options like -c to display a count of the number of times each line appears, or -d to display only the duplicate lines.

Counting the number of lines, words, or characters in a text file: You can use the wc command to count the number of lines, words, or characters in a text file. The wc command reads a file or stream of data and counts the number of lines, words, and characters. You can use options like -l to count the number of lines, -w to count the number of words, or -c to count the number of characters.

Splitting a text file into smaller files: You can use the split command to split a large text file into smaller files, based on the number of lines or the size of the files. The split command reads a file or stream of data and divides it into a specified number of smaller files. You can use options like -l to specify the number of lines per file, or -b to specify the size of the files in bytes.

Using 'grep'

Following is an example of how to use the grep command to search for patterns of text in a file:

Suppose you have a file called data.txt that contains the following lines:

```
apple
banana
cherry
date
elderberry
fig
```

You can use the grep command to search for a specific word or phrase in the file, like this:

```
grep cherry data.txt
```

This will display the following output:

```
cherry
```

The grep command searches for the pattern "cherry" in the data.txt file and displays the lines that match.

You can also use regular expressions to search for more complex patterns of text. For example, to search for lines that contain the letter "e" anywhere in the line, you can use the following command:

```
grep e data.txt
```

This will display the following output:

```
apple
date
elderberry
```

You can use options like -i to ignore case, -v to display non-matching lines, or -n to display line numbers. For example, to search for lines that do not contain the letter "e" and display the line numbers, you can use the following command:

```
grep -v -n e data.txt
```

This will display the following output:

```
2:banana
3:cherry
5:fig
```

Using 'nl'

Following is an example of how to use the nl command to display a text file with line numbers:

Suppose you have a file called data.txt that contains the following lines:

```
apple
```

```
banana
cherry
date
elderberry
fig
```

You can use the nl command to display the file with line numbers, like this:

```
nl data.txt
```

This will display the following output:

```
     1  apple
     2  banana
     3  cherry
     4  date
     5  elderberry
     6  fig
```

The nl command reads the data.txt file and adds line numbers to the beginning of each line.

You can use options like -b to specify the type of line numbering to use (such as "t" for non-empty lines or "a" for all lines), or -n to specify the starting line number. For example, to number only the non-empty lines and start with line number 10, you can use the following command:

```
nl -bt -n 10 data.txt
```

This will display the following output:

```
    10  apple
```

```
11    banana
12    cherry
13    date
14    elderberry
15    fig
```

Using 'tail'

Following is an example of how to use the tail command to display the last few lines of a text file:

Suppose you have a file called data.txt that contains the following lines:

```
apple
banana
cherry
date
elderberry
fig
grape
huckleberry
```

You can use the tail command to display the last few lines of the file, like this:

```
tail data.txt
```

This will display the following output:

```
elderberry
fig
grape
huckleberry
```

By default, the tail command displays the last 10 lines of the file. You can use the -n option to specify a different number of lines to display. For example, to display the last 5 lines of the file, you can use the following command:

```
tail -n 5 data.txt
```

This will display the following output:

```
cherry
date
elderberry
fig
grape
```

You can also use the -f option to follow the file as it grows. This is useful for monitoring log files or other files that are continuously updated. For example, to display the last 10 lines of the data.txt file and follow it as it grows, you can use the following command:

```
tail -f data.txt
```

Using 'head'

Following is another example of how to use the head command to display the first few lines of a text file:

Suppose you have a file called data.csv that contains a large dataset with thousands of rows and columns. You can use the head command to display the first few lines of the file to get a sense of the data that it contains:

```
head data.csv
```

This will display the first few lines of the file, which might look something like this:

```
id,name,age,gender,income
1,Alice,25,Female,55000
2,Bob,32,Male,60000
3,Charlie,28,Male,52000
4,Diana,30,Female,67000
5,Eve,27,Female,57000
```

The head command is useful for quickly previewing the contents of a large file without having to open it in a text editor or spreadsheet program.

You can also use the head command in combination with other tools to perform operations on the data. For example, you can use the cut command to extract specific columns of data from the file, like this:

```
head data.csv | cut -d , -f 2
```

This will display the second column of data (the "name" column) from the first few lines of the file:

```
name
Alice
Bob
Charlie
```

```
Diana
Eve
```

Using 'sed'

Following is an example of how to use the sed command to search and replace patterns of text in a file:

Suppose you have a file called data.txt that contains the following lines:

```
apple
banana
cherry
date
elderberry
fig
```

You can use the sed command to search for a specific word or phrase and replace it with another word or phrase, like this:

```
sed 's/apple/orange/' data.txt
```

This will display the following output:

```
orange
banana
cherry
date
```

```
elderberry
fig
```

The sed command reads the data.txt file and searches for the pattern "apple". When it finds a match, it replaces it with the string "orange".

You can use regular expressions to search for more complex patterns of text. For example, to search for lines that contain the letter "e" anywhere in the line and replace them with the string "X", you can use the following command:

```
sed 's/e/X/g' data.txt
```

This will display the following output:

```
applX
banana
chXrry
datX
XldXrberry
fig
```

You can also use the -i option to edit the file in place, rather than displaying the output to the terminal. For example, to search for the string "cherry" and replace it with the string "peach" in the data.txt file, you can use the following command:

```
sed -i 's/cherry/peach/'
```

This will modify the data.txt file so that it now contains the following lines:

```
apple
banana
```

```
peach
date
elderberry
fig
```

You can also use the sed command to perform more advanced transformations on the text data. For example, you can use the p flag to print only certain lines that match a pattern, or the d flag to delete certain lines that match a pattern.

For example, to print only the lines that contain the letter "e", you can use the following command:

```
sed -n '/e/p' data.txt
```

This will display the following output:

```
apple
date
elderberry
```

To delete the lines that contain the letter "e", you can use the following command:

```
sed '/e/d' data.txt
```

This will display the following output:

```
banana
cherry
fig
```

Using 'more' and 'less'

Following is an example of how to use the more and less commands to view the contents of a text file:

Suppose you have a file called data.txt that contains a large amount of data, more than can fit on a single screen. You can use the more or less commands to view the contents of the file one screen at a time.

To view the contents of the data.txt file using the more command, you can use the following command:

```
more data.txt
```

This will display the first screen of the file, and you can use the space bar to advance to the next screen, or the q key to quit.

To view the contents of the data.txt file using the less command, you can use the following command:

```
less data.txt
```

This will display the first screen of the file, and you can use the up and down arrow keys to navigate through the file, or the q key to quit.

Both more and less allow you to search for specific patterns of text within the file. To search for a specific pattern using more, you can use the forward slash (/) followed by the pattern, like this:

```
/pattern
```

For example, to search for the word "apple" in the data.txt file using more, you can use the following command:

```
/apple
```

To search for a specific pattern using less, you can use the forward slash (/) followed by the pattern, like this:

```
/pattern
```

For example, to search for the word "apple" in the data.txt file using less, you can use the following command:

```
/apple
```

Summary

Following is a summary of some of the key concepts related to text manipulation using the command line:

The grep command is used to search for patterns of text in a file or stream of data. It can be used with regular expressions to search for complex patterns, and has options to ignore case, display non-matching lines, or display line numbers.

The nl command is used to display a text file with line numbers. It has options to specify the type of line numbering to use (such as "t" for non-empty lines or "a" for all lines) and the starting line number.

The tail command is used to display the last few lines of a text file. It has options to specify the number of lines to display and to follow the file as it grows.

The head command is used to display the first few lines of a text file. It has options to specify the number of lines to display and to suppress the output of file names when reading multiple files.

The sed command is used to search and replace patterns of text in a file. It can be used with regular expressions to search for complex patterns, and has options to edit the file in place, print only certain lines, or delete certain lines.

The more and less commands are used to view the contents of a text file one screen at a time. Both commands have options to search for specific patterns of text within the file.

Hack#1: Searching Complex Pattern

Suppose you have a file called data.txt that contains the following lines:

```
apple
banana
cherry
date
elderberry
fig
```

You can use regular expressions to search for a pattern that matches any line that contains the letter "e", like this:

```
grep 'e' data.txt
```

This will display the following output:

```
apple
date
elderberry
```

Hack#2: Editing Files

Suppose you want to search for the word "apple" and replace it with the word "orange" in the data.txt file. You can use the sed command with the -i option to edit the file in place, like this:

```
sed -i 's/apple/orange/' data.txt
```

This will modify the data.txt file so that it now contains the following lines:

```
orange
banana
cherry
date
elderberry
fig
```

Hack#3: Specify Starting Line Number

Suppose you have a file called data.txt that contains the following lines:

```
apple
banana
cherry
date
elderberry
fig
```

You can use the nl command with the -n option to number the lines starting from a specific number, like this:

```
nl -n 5 data.txt
```

This will display the following output:

```
     5  apple
     6  banana
     7  cherry
     8  date
     9  elderberry
    10  fig
```

Hack#4: Monitoring Files

Suppose you have a file called log.txt that is being continuously updated with new lines of data. You can use the tail command with the -f option to follow the file as it grows, like this:

```
tail -f log.txt
```

This will display the last few lines of the file, and then update the display as new lines are added to the file.

Hack#5: Combining Text Commands

Suppose you have a file called data.csv that contains a large dataset with thousands of rows and columns, and you want to extract the second column of data (the "name" column) and save it to a new file called names.txt. You can use the grep and cut commands together with piping and redirection to do this, like this:

```
grep '^[^,]*,[^,]*,.*' data.csv | cut -d , -f 2 > names.txt
```

This will extract the second column of data from the data.csv file and save it to the names.txt file.

CHAPTER 3: ADMINISTERING NETWORKS

Overview of Network-Related Commands

Purpose of Network Related Commands

The purpose of network related commands in Linux is to allow you to view and manipulate various aspects of your system's network configuration and connectivity. For example, you can use the ifconfig command to view and set the IP address and netmask of a network interface, or the ping command to test connectivity between two devices on a network.

Other network related commands allow you to view and manipulate the IP routing table (route), display information about active network connections (netstat), or query the Domain Name System (DNS) to resolve domain names to IP addresses (nslookup).

Overall, these commands provide a means of interacting with and managing your system's network configuration and connectivity, which is important for maintaining a stable and functional network.

Advantages of Network Commands

There are several advantages to using network related commands in Linux:

Flexibility: Network commands allow you to view and manipulate various aspects of your system's network configuration and connectivity. This allows you to fine-tune your system's network settings to meet your specific needs.

Diagnostics: Network commands can be useful for diagnosing and troubleshooting network connectivity issues. For example, you can use the ping command to test connectivity between two devices, or the traceroute command to trace the path taken by packets over an IP network.

Scripting: Network commands can be used in scripts to automate network tasks. This can be particularly useful for managing large networks or performing repetitive tasks.

Command line interface: Network commands are typically run from the command line, which can be more efficient than using a graphical user interface (GUI) for certain tasks.

Overall, network commands are a powerful and flexible tool for managing and troubleshooting your system's network configuration and connectivity.

Examples of Network Commands:

ifconfig: This command is used to configure network interface parameters. With it, you can view and set the IP address, netmask, and broadcast address of a network interface, as well as enable or disable the interface.

ping: This command is used to test the connectivity between two devices on a network. It works by sending a small data packet to a remote device, and measuring the time it takes for the packet to be returned.

traceroute: This command is used to trace the path taken by packets over an IP network. It can be useful for troubleshooting network connectivity issues.

netstat: This command is used to display information about active network connections and routing tables. It can show you the status of TCP and UDP connections, as well as the addresses and states of the sockets being used.

route: This command is used to view and manipulate the IP routing table. With it, you can add, delete, or modify entries in the routing table.

nslookup: This command is used to query the Domain Name System (DNS) to obtain domain name or IP address mappings, or to find the name servers responsible for a particular domain.

Using 'ifconfig'

The ifconfig command is used to configure network interface parameters in Kali Linux. Following is an example of how to use it:

Open a terminal window.

Type ifconfig and press Enter. This will display a list of your system's network interfaces, along with their current configuration.

To view the configuration of a specific interface, you can use the following syntax:

```
ifconfig <interface>
```

For example, to view the configuration of the eth0 interface, you would type:

```
ifconfig eth0
```

This will display the current configuration of the eth0 interface, including the IP address, netmask, and broadcast address.

To set the IP address of an interface, you can use the following syntax:

```
ifconfig <interface> <IP address>
```

For example, to set the IP address of the eth0 interface to 192.168.1.100, you would type:

```
ifconfig eth0 192.168.1.100
```

To set the netmask of an interface, you can use the following syntax:

```
ifconfig <interface> netmask <netmask>
```

For example, to set the netmask of the eth0 interface to 255.255.255.0, you would type:

```
ifconfig eth0 netmask 255.255.255.0
```

Using 'iwconfig'

The iwconfig command is used to configure wireless network interfaces in Kali Linux. Following is an example of how to use it:

Open a terminal window.

Type iwconfig and press Enter. This will display a list of your system's wireless interfaces, along with their current configuration.

To view the configuration of a specific wireless interface, you can use the following syntax:

```
iwconfig <interface>
```

For example, to view the configuration of the wlan0 interface, you would type:

```
iwconfig wlan0
```

This will display the current configuration of the wlan0 interface, including the wireless mode, channel, and ESSID.

To set the wireless mode of an interface, you can use the following syntax:

```
iwconfig <interface> mode <mode>
```

For example, to set the wireless mode of the wlan0 interface to managed, you would type:

```
iwconfig wlan0 mode managed
```

To set the wireless channel of an interface, you can use the following syntax:

```
iwconfig <interface> channel <channel>
```

For example, to set the wireless channel of the wlan0 interface to 6, you would type:

```
iwconfig wlan0 channel 6
```

To set the ESSID (network name) of an interface, you can use the following syntax:

```
iwconfig <interface> essid <ESSID>
```

For example, to set the ESSID of the wlan0 interface to MyNetwork, you would type:

```
iwconfig wlan0 essid MyNetwork
```

Using 'dig'

The dig command is a tool for querying the Domain Name System (DNS) in Kali Linux. Following is an example of how to use it:

Open a terminal window.

Type dig followed by the domain name you want to look up, and press Enter. For example, to look up the IP address for the domain example.com, you would type:

```
dig example.com
```

This will return the IP address associated with the domain name example.com.

You can also use the dig command to perform specific types of DNS queries. For example, to perform a reverse DNS lookup (mapping an IP address to a domain name), you can use the following syntax:

```
dig -x <IP address>
```

For example, to perform a reverse DNS lookup for the IP address 192.0.2.1, you would type:

```
dig -x 192.0.2.1
```

This will return the domain name associated with the IP address 192.0.2.1.

You can also specify the DNS server to use for the query using the @ symbol, like this:

```
dig <domain> @<server>
```

For example, to perform a DNS lookup for the domain example.com using the DNS server 8.8.8.8, you would type:

```
dig example.com @8.8.8.8
```

Using 'traceroute'

The traceroute command is a tool for tracing the path taken by packets over an IP network in Kali Linux. Following is an example of how to use it:

Open a terminal window.

Type traceroute followed by the domain name or IP address of the destination you want to trace the path to, and press Enter. For example, to trace the path to the domain example.com, you would type:

```
traceroute example.com
```

This will display the list of hops taken by the packets to reach the destination, along with the round-trip time (RTT) for each hop.

You can also specify the maximum number of hops to trace using the -m option, like this:

```
traceroute -m <hops> <destination>
```

For example, to trace the path to the domain example.com with a maximum of 10 hops, you would type:

```
traceroute -m 10 example.com
```

You can also specify the port number to use for the trace using the -p option, like this:

```
traceroute -p <port> <destination>
```

For example, to trace the path to the domain example.com using port 80, you would type:

```
traceroute -p 80 example.com
```

Using 'netstat'

The netstat command is a tool for displaying information about active network connections and routing tables in Kali Linux. Following is an example of how to use it:

Open a terminal window.

Type netstat and press Enter. This will display a list of active network connections, along with their state, local and remote addresses, and the process ID of the program associated with the connection.

You can also use the -a option to display all active connections, including those in the listening state:

```
netstat -a
```

To display only the connections for a specific protocol, you can use the -p option followed by the protocol name, like this:

```
netstat -p <protocol>
```

For example, to display only the TCP connections, you would type:

```
netstat -p tcp
```

You can also use the -r option to display the kernel routing table:

```
netstat -r
```

Using 'nslookup'

The nslookup command is a tool for querying the Domain Name System (DNS) in Kali Linux. Following is an example of how to use it:

Open a terminal window.

Type nslookup followed by the domain name you want to look up, and press Enter. For example, to look up the IP address for the domain example.com, you would type:
nslookup example.com

This will return the IP address associated with the domain name example.com.

You can also use the nslookup command to perform a reverse DNS lookup (mapping an IP address to a domain name). To do this, use the following syntax:

```
nslookup <IP address>
```

For example, to perform a reverse DNS lookup for the IP address 192.0.2.1, you would type:

```
nslookup 192.0.2.1
```

This will return the domain name associated with the IP address 192.0.2.1.

You can also specify the DNS server to use for the query using the server command, like this:

```
nslookup
> server <server>
> <domain>
```

For example, to perform a DNS lookup for the domain example.com using the DNS server 8.8.8.8, you would type:

```
nslookup
```

```
> server 8.8.8.8
> example.com
```

Searching Wireless Devices

Searching for wireless devices refers to the process of finding and identifying wireless networks that are within range of your device. This can be useful if you want to connect to a wireless network or gather information about the available networks in an area.

In Kali Linux, you can use the iwlist command to scan for wireless networks. The iwlist command displays detailed information about the wireless interfaces on your system, including the available wireless networks.

To use the iwlist command, you first need to make sure that your wireless interface is up. You can use the ifconfig command to check the status of your wireless interface. If it is down, you can use the following command to bring it up:

Using 'iwlist'

To search for wireless devices in Kali Linux using the iwlist command, following are the steps to follow:

Open a terminal window.

Make sure your wireless interface is up. You can use the ifconfig command to check the status of your wireless interface. If it is down, use the following command to bring it up:

```
ifconfig <interface> up
```

Replace <interface> with the name of your wireless interface (e.g. wlan0).

Scan for wireless networks using the iwlist command. Use the following syntax:

```
iwlist <interface> scan
```

Replace <interface> with the name of your wireless interface (e.g. wlan0).

This will scan for wireless networks in range and display a list of the available networks, including their SSID (network name), frequency, and encryption type.

Connect to a wireless network using the iwconfig command. Use the following syntax:

```
iwconfig <interface> essid <SSID> key <key>
```

Replace <interface> with the name of your wireless interface (e.g. wlan0), <SSID> with the network name of the wireless network you want to connect to, and <key> with the network key (password).

For example, to connect to a wireless network with the SSID MyNetwork and the key password123, you would type:

```
iwconfig wlan0 essid MyNetwork key password123
```

Verify that you are connected to the wireless network by using the iwconfig command again. The output should show that the wireless interface is associated with the SSID of the network you are connected to.

Modifying IPv4 Addresses

Understanding IPv4

An IPv4 address is a numerical label assigned to each device connected to a computer network that uses the Internet Protocol for communication. An IPv4 address is a 32-bit number that uniquely identifies a network interface on a device. It is usually written in dot-decimal notation, with four octets separated by periods (e.g. 192.0.2.1).

IPv4 addresses are divided into two parts: the network prefix and the host identifier. The network prefix identifies the network to which the device belongs, and the host identifier identifies the device within the network. The number of bits in the network prefix and the host identifier varies depending on the subnet mask used for the network.

IPv4 addresses are hierarchical, which means that they are organized into a hierarchy of networks and subnetworks. This allows devices on different networks to communicate with each other through routers, which forward packets between networks.

IPv4 addresses are being replaced by IPv6 addresses, which are longer and provide a much larger address space. However, IPv4 addresses are still widely used and are likely to remain in use for some time.

Popular IPv4 Related Commands

Following is a list of some common commands used for working with IPv4 addresses in Linux:

ifconfig - This command is used to view and set the IP address, netmask, and broadcast address of a network interface.

ip - This command is a newer tool that provides similar functionality to ifconfig, but with a more flexible syntax.

route - This command is used to view and manipulate the IP routing table, which determines how packets are forwarded between networks.

netstat - This command is used to display information about active network connections and the status of various network protocols.

ping - This command is used to test connectivity between two devices on a network by sending an ICMP echo request and waiting for a reply.

traceroute - This command is used to trace the path taken by packets over an IP network.

nslookup - This command is used to query the Domain Name System (DNS) to resolve domain names to IP addresses.

dig - This command is similar to nslookup, but is more powerful and has a more flexible syntax.

Modifying The Addresses (IPv4)

To modify the IPv4 address of a network interface in Linux, you can use the ifconfig or ip command. Following is an example of how to use the ifconfig command to set the IP address of the eth0 interface to 192.168.1.100:

```
ifconfig eth0 192.168.1.100
```

To set the netmask of the eth0 interface to 255.255.255.0, you can use the following command:

```
ifconfig eth0 netmask 255.255.255.0
```

To set the broadcast address of the eth0 interface to 192.168.1.255, you can use the following command:

```
ifconfig eth0 broadcast 192.168.1.255
```

You can also use the ip command to modify the IPv4 address of a network interface. The ip command has a more flexible syntax and provides additional features, such as the ability to set multiple addresses and routes on a single interface.

Following is an example of how to use the ip command to set the IP address of the eth0 interface to 192.168.1.100:

```
ip address add 192.168.1.100/24 dev eth0
```

This will add the IP address 192.168.1.100 to the eth0 interface with a netmask of 255.255.255.0 (indicated by the /24 part of the command).

To set the default route for the eth0 interface, you can use the following command:

```
ip route add default via 192.168.1.1 dev eth0
```

To modify the IPv4 address of a network interface in Linux, you can also use the ip command with the addr subcommand. Following is an example of how to use the ip command to set the IP address of the eth0 interface to 192.168.1.100:

```
ip addr add 192.168.1.100/24 dev eth0
```

This will add the IP address 192.168.1.100 to the eth0 interface with a netmask of 255.255.255.0 (indicated by the /24 part of the command).

To set the default route for the eth0 interface, you can use the following command:

```
ip route add default via 192.168.1.1 dev eth0
```

You can also use the ip command with the addr subcommand to delete an IP address from an interface. To delete the IP address 192.168.1.100 from the eth0 interface, you can use the following command:

```
ip addr del 192.168.1.100/24 dev eth0
```

Modifying IPv6 Addresses

Following is an example of how you might use the ifconfig and ip commands to modify IPv6 addresses on a Linux system.

Suppose you have a server with the IPv6 address 2001:db8:0:1::10/64 on the eth0 interface, and you want to change the address to 2001:db8:0:1::20/64. Here are the steps you could follow:

Open a terminal window and log in to the server.

Use the ifconfig command to delete the existing IPv6 address from the eth0 interface:

```
ifconfig eth0 inet6 del 2001:db8:0:1::10/64
```

Use the ifconfig command to add the new IPv6 address to the eth0 interface:

```
ifconfig eth0 inet6 add 2001:db8:0:1::20/64
```

Alternatively, you can use the ip command with the addr subcommand to delete the existing IPv6 address and add the new one in a single command:

```
ip -6 addr replace 2001:db8:0:1::20/64 dev eth0
```

Use the ping6 command to test connectivity with the new IPv6 address:

```
ping6 2001:db8:0:1::20
```

If the ping is successful, then the new IPv6 address has been successfully set on the eth0 interface.

Deleting IP Address

To delete an IPv6 address using ifconfig, use the following syntax:

```
ifconfig <interface> inet6 del <IPv6 address>
```

Replace <interface> with the name of the network interface (e.g. eth0) and <IPv6 address> with the IPv6 address you want to delete (e.g. 2001:db8:0:1::1/64).

For example, to delete the IPv6 address 2001:db8:0:1::1/64 from the eth0 interface, you would type:

```
ifconfig eth0 inet6 del 2001:db8:0:1::1/64
```

To delete an IPv6 address using ip, use the following syntax:

```
ip -6 addr del <IPv6 address> dev <interface>
```

Replace <IPv6 address> with the IPv6 address you want to delete (e.g. 2001:db8:0:1::1/64) and <interface> with the name of the network interface (e.g. eth0).

For example, to delete the IPv6 address 2001:db8:0:1::1/64 from the eth0 interface, you would type:

```
ip -6 addr del 2001:db8:0:1::1/64 dev eth0
```

Cloning IP Addresses

What Is Cloning of IP Address?

IP address cloning is the process of assigning a device multiple IP addresses that belong to different network interfaces. This can be done for various reasons, such as to allow a device to communicate with multiple networks simultaneously or to bypass IP address restrictions.

There are several ways to clone an IP address, depending on the operating system and network architecture being used. In some cases, it may be possible to clone an IP address by assigning it to a virtual network interface, such as a virtual machine or a virtual private network (VPN) connection. In other cases, it may be necessary to use network address translation (NAT) or proxy servers to route traffic between the device and the multiple networks.

It is important to note that cloning an IP address may violate network policies and can potentially cause conflicts or security issues. As such, it is generally recommended to use other methods, such as network address translation or virtual network interfaces, to communicate with multiple networks instead of cloning an IP address.

Steps To Clone IP

There are several ways to clone an IP address, and the specific steps will depend on the operating system and network architecture being used. Here are some general steps that may be involved in the process:

- Determine the IP address that you want to clone and the network interface that you want to use for the cloning.

- Determine whether the operating system and network architecture support IP address cloning. Some systems may not allow multiple IP addresses to be assigned to the same network interface, or may require the use of virtual network interfaces or network address translation to achieve the same effect.

- Configure the network interface to use the IP address that you want to clone. This may involve modifying the network settings or adding the IP address to the interface using a command-line tool.

- Test the IP address cloning to make sure that it is working as intended. This may involve pinging other devices on the network or trying to connect to other networks using the cloned IP address.

- Monitor the network for any issues or conflicts that may arise as a result of the IP address cloning.

It is important to note that cloning an IP address may violate network policies and can potentially cause conflicts or security issues. As such, it is generally recommended to use other methods, such as network address translation or virtual network interfaces, to communicate with multiple networks instead of cloning an IP address.

How To Clone The IP Address

Following is an example of how you might clone an IP address on a Linux system using a virtual network interface:

Determine the IP address that you want to clone and the network interface that you want to use for the cloning. For this example, let's say that you want to clone the IP address 192.168.1.100 and use the eth0 interface.

Create a virtual network interface using the ip command. For example:

```
ip link add link eth0 name eth0:1 type macvlan
```

This will create a virtual network interface named eth0:1 that is linked to the eth0 interface.

Assign the IP address that you want to clone to the virtual network interface. For example:

```
ifconfig eth0:1 192.168.1.100
```

This will assign the IP address 192.168.1.100 to the virtual network interface eth0:1.

Test the IP address cloning to make sure that it is working as intended. You can do this by pinging other devices on the network or trying to connect to other networks using the cloned IP address.

Monitor the network for any issues or conflicts that may arise as a result of the IP address cloning.

Considerations While Cloning IP

Here are some additional considerations to keep in mind when cloning an IP address:

- Make sure that the IP address you want to clone is not already in use on the network. If another device is already using the same IP address, it can cause conflicts and connectivity issues.
- Be aware of any network policies or restrictions that may prohibit the use of IP address cloning. Some networks may have strict rules about the assignment of IP addresses, and cloning an IP address may violate these policies.
- Consider the security implications of cloning an IP address. Cloning an IP address can make it more difficult to track network activity, and may make it easier for an attacker to gain unauthorized access to the network.
- Monitor the network for any issues or conflicts that may arise as a result of the IP address cloning. If you notice any connectivity issues or other problems, you may need to modify the network settings or disable the cloned IP address.

Phishing MAC Address

What is Phishing?

Phishing is a type of cybercrime in which attackers use fake websites, emails, or text messages to trick people into disclosing sensitive information, such as passwords, credit card numbers, or bank account numbers.

The attackers typically create a fake website or email that looks legitimate and includes a link or a form that asks the user to enter personal information. When the user clicks on the link or submits the form, their information is sent to the attackers, who can then use it to gain access to their accounts or steal their identity.

Phishing attacks can be difficult to detect, as the fake websites and emails are often designed to look very similar to the real ones. To protect yourself from phishing attacks, you should be cautious when clicking on links or entering personal information online, and you should be suspicious of any emails or text messages that ask for sensitive information or contain unusual requests. It's also a good idea to use strong passwords and to enable two factor authentication for your online accounts.

Phishing of MAC Address

Phishing a MAC (Media Access Control) address refers to the practice of tricking someone into revealing the MAC address of their device. A MAC address is a unique identifier assigned to every device on a network, and it can be used to identify and track the device.

There are several ways that an attacker could attempt to phish a MAC address. For example, they might send a fake email or text message claiming to be from a legitimate company and asking the user to provide their MAC address for troubleshooting purposes. Alternatively, they might create a fake website that asks the user to enter their MAC address in order to access a particular service or feature.

Phishing a MAC address is not a common type of attack, as MAC addresses are not typically considered sensitive information and are not typically used to access accounts or services. However, an attacker could potentially use a phished MAC address to track a device or to perform other types of attacks, such as sniffing network traffic or performing man-in-the-middle attacks.

To protect yourself from MAC address phishing attacks, you should be cautious when providing personal information online and be suspicious of any requests for your MAC address. It's also a good idea to use strong passwords and to enable two-factor authentication for your online accounts to protect yourself from other types of cyber threats.

How to Phish MAC Address

Following is an example of how an attacker might attempt this type of attack:

- The attacker creates a fake website or email that appears to be from a legitimate company, such as a computer manufacturer or an internet service provider.
- The fake website or email includes a link or a form that asks the user to enter their MAC address for troubleshooting purposes or to access a particular service or feature.
- The user clicks on the link or submits the form, thinking that they are communicating with a legitimate company.
- The attacker receives the MAC address from the user and can use it to track the device or perform other types of attacks.

This is just one example of how an attacker might attempt to phish a MAC address. There are many other ways that an attacker could try to trick someone into revealing their MAC address, and the specific methods used will depend on the resources and skills of the attacker.

Accessing DNS

Methods of Accessing DNS

Several ways to access Domain Name System (DNS) records on a computer or network. Some common methods include:

- Using the nslookup command: This is a command-line tool that allows you to query DNS servers for information about a domain or hostname. To use nslookup, open a terminal or command prompt and type nslookup <domain or hostname>. For example, to look up the DNS records for www.example.com, you would type nslookup www.example.com.

- Using the dig command: This is another command-line tool that allows you to query DNS servers for information about a domain or hostname. To use dig, open a terminal or command prompt and type dig <domain or hostname>. For example, to look up the DNS records for www.example.com, you would type dig www.example.com.

- Using a web-based DNS lookup tool: There are many websites that allow you to look up DNS records by entering a domain or hostname. Some popular options include DNS Lookup (https://www.whatsmydns.net/dns-lookup.html) and DNS Checker (https://dnschecker.org/).

- Using the host command: This is a command-line tool that allows you to look up DNS records for a domain or hostname. To use host, open a terminal or command prompt and type host <domain or hostname>. For example, to look up the DNS records for www.example.com, you would type host www.example.com.

Evaluating DNS Server

Need of DNS Evaluation

Several reasons why you might want to evaluate DNS records:

Troubleshooting: If you are experiencing connectivity issues or other problems with a domain or hostname, evaluating the DNS records can help you identify the cause of the problem and find a solution.

Security: DNS records can contain sensitive information, such as the IP addresses of servers or the locations of domain names. Evaluating DNS records can help you identify any potential security risks or vulnerabilities.

Performance: Evaluating DNS records can help you optimize the performance of your website or network. For example, you might check the DNS records to ensure that your website is using a fast and reliable DNS provider, or to make sure that your network is using the most efficient DNS servers.

Compliance: Some organizations may have strict policies or regulations about the use of DNS records, and evaluating the records can help you ensure that you are in compliance with these policies.

Steps to Evaluate DNS Server

There are several ways to evaluate DNS servers, and the specific steps will depend on your goals and the tools that you are using. Here are some general steps that you might follow to evaluate a DNS server:

- Determine the DNS server that you want to evaluate. You can do this by looking up the DNS records for a domain or hostname using a command-line tool like nslookup or dig, or by using a web-based DNS lookup tool.

- Test the DNS server's performance. You can use tools like dig or nslookup to measure the time it takes for the DNS server to resolve a domain or hostname. You can also use a tool like dnsperf or resperf to test the server's performance under different workloads and conditions.

- Check the DNS server's security. You can use tools like dnssec-tools or dnssec-analyze to check the DNS server's security settings and configurations. You can also use a tool like sslyze to test the server's SSL/TLS security.

- Check the DNS server's compliance with policies or regulations. If you are required to adhere to specific policies or regulations regarding DNS servers, you can use tools like dnssec-policy or dnssec-compliance to check the server's compliance.

- Monitor the DNS server for any issues or problems. You can use tools like dns-monitor or dnstap to monitor the server for any issues or problems, such as connectivity issues or security vulnerabilities.

Modifying DNS Server

Ways To Modify DNS Server

There are several ways to modify a DNS server, depending on the operating system and network architecture being used. Here are some general steps that you might follow to modify a DNS server:

- Determine the DNS server that you want to modify. This might be a local DNS server on your network, or it might be a remote DNS server provided by your internet service provider (ISP) or a third-party DNS provider.

- Identify the settings or configurations that you want to modify. This might include the IP address of the DNS server, the DNS records that it maintains, or the security settings for the server.

- Access the DNS server's configuration interface. This might be a web-based interface, a command-line tool, or a configuration file on the server.
- Make the necessary changes to the DNS server's settings or configurations. This might involve modifying the IP address of the DNS server, adding or removing DNS records, or changing the security settings for the server.
- Save the changes and test the modified DNS server to make sure that it is working as intended. This might involve pinging the DNS server or using a command-line tool like dig or nslookup to query the server for information.

It is important to be careful when modifying a DNS server, as incorrect configurations can cause connectivity issues or other problems.

Hack#1: Subnetting

In Linux, you can use the "ip" command to perform subnetting calculations. The "ip" command allows you to view and configure various network settings, including IP addresses and subnet masks. For example, the following command can be used to display the IP address and subnet mask of a network interface:

```
ip addr show eth0
```

You can also use the "ip" command to change the IP address and subnet mask of a network interface, for example:

```
ip addr add 192.168.1.100/24 dev eth0
```

Hack#2: Use of EUI-64 Format

Using EUI-64 format: In Linux, you can use the "ip" command to generate EUI-64 addresses from the MAC addresses of network interfaces. For example, the following command generates a unique EUI-64 address for the network interface "eth0":

```
ip link set dev eth0 address 00:11:22:33:44:55/64
```

Hack#3: Finding MAC Address

In Linux, you can use the "ifconfig" command to find the MAC address of a network interface. The following command will display the MAC address of the "eth0" interface:

```
ifconfig eth0
```

Hack#4: DNS Troubleshooting

The "nslookup" command in Linux is a useful tool for troubleshooting DNS issues. This command allows you to query DNS servers for information about a specific domain name, for example:

```
nslookup example.com
```

Hack#5: DNS Caching

To speed up name resolution and reduce the load on DNS servers, Linux systems use a local DNS cache called nscd. You can use the "nscd" command to manage the DNS cache, for example:

```
service nscd status
```

This command will show the status of the nscd service and you can use it to start, stop or restart the service as well.

CHAPTER 4: ADD AND DELETE APPLICATIONS

Overview of Package Management System

When it comes to installing, updating, and removing software packages, Linux distributions typically use one of several different package management systems. These systems can be found in the Linux distribution's official repositories. Some examples include:

- apt (Advanced Package Tool) - used in Debian and Ubuntu-based distributions
- yum (Yellowdog Updater, Modified) - used in Red Hat, CentOS, and Fedora-based distributions
- dnf (Dandified Yum) - a fork of yum used in newer versions of Fedora
- zypper - used in SUSE and openSUSE-based distributions
- pacman - used in Arch Linux and its derivatives

apt

apt-get install - install a package (or a group of packages)
apt-get remove - remove a package (leaves configuration files behind)
apt-get purge - remove a package and its configuration files
apt-get update - update the package index files from the package repositories
apt-get upgrade - upgrade all installed packages to their latest versions

yum

yum install - install a package (or a group of packages)
yum remove - remove a package (leaves configuration files behind)
yum erase - remove a package and its configuration files
yum update - update all installed packages to their latest versions
yum check-update - check for available updates

dnf

dnf install - install a package (or a group of packages)
dnf remove - remove a package (leaves configuration files behind)
dnf erase - remove a package and its configuration files
dnf update - update all installed packages to their latest versions
dnf check-update - check for available updates

zypper

zypper install - install a package (or a group of packages)
zypper remove - remove a package
zypper update - update all installed packages to their latest versions
zypper list-updates - list available updates

pacman

pacman -S - install a package (or a group of packages)
pacman -R - remove a package (leaves configuration files behind)
pacman -Rs - remove a package and its configuration files
pacman -Sy - synchronize the package database with the package repositories
pacman -Su - upgrade all installed packages to their latest versions

Using GUI Installers

GUI Programs

Installing software on a Linux computer can be done with the help of graphical user interface (GUI) installers, which are programs with a graphical user interface. When compared to using the command line, these programs offer a method of installing software that is more user-friendly. This makes the process simpler for users who either are not familiar with the command line or who prefer a more visual interface.

The following is a list of some of the more popular graphical user interface (GUI) installers that can be found in various Linux distributions:

- Software Center is a graphical user interface application that enables users to browse, install, and remove software packages from a list of available applications. This application is included with many distributions that are based on Ubuntu.

- GNOME Software is a graphical user interface application that is bundled with numerous distributions, including Fedora and CentOS, that make use of the GNOME desktop environment. It provides users with the ability to browse, install, and uninstall software packages from a list of applications that are available.

- KDE Discover is a graphical user interface (GUI) application that is bundled with a variety of distributions, including openSUSE, that make use of the KDE desktop environment. It gives users the ability to browse through a list of available applications, install or remove software packages, and remove software packages from their computer.

- App Store is a graphical user interface (GUI) application that is included with some distributions, such as elementary OS, and that enables users to browse, install, and remove software packages from a list of available applications.

In addition to these GUI installers, many Linux distributions also include a package manager that can be used to install software from the command line. Installing a separate application that provides a graphical frontend for the package manager is required in order to use these package managers, such as apt or yum, to install software through a graphical user interface. This is something that must be done in order to successfully complete this task.

Use 'apt' to Manage Programs

On Linux distributions based on Ubuntu and Debian, apt, also known as the Advanced Package Tool, is a package management system that allows users to install, update, and remove software packages. The following is a list of examples illustrating how you can use apt to install, modify, and remove software:

Installing Package

You can use the apt install subcommand and give it the name of the package you want to install in order to perform a single-package installation using apt. Take, for instance:

```
sudo apt-get install package-name
```

You also have the option of installing multiple packages simultaneously by providing a list of package names that are separated by spaces:

```
sudo apt-get install package-name-1 package-name-2 package-name-3
```

Updating Package

You can use the upgrade subcommand to bring all of your installed packages up to date with the most recent versions that are available in the package repositories:

```
sudo apt-get upgrade
```

Removing Package

You can remove a single package from your system using apt by using the remove subcommand and providing the name of the package you wish to remove as the argument. The configuration files for the package will be left behind as a result of this action:

```
sudo apt-get remove package-name
```

To remove a package and its configuration files, you can use the purge subcommand:

```
sudo apt-get purge package-name
```

You can also remove multiple packages at the same time by specifying a list of package names separated by spaces:

```
sudo apt-get remove package-name-1 package-name-2 package-name-3
```

It is important to keep in mind that the preceding are merely a few examples of the numerous options and subcommands that can be used with apt. You can find more information about using apt by consulting the apt-get man page or the documentation for your specific Linux distribution.

Finding Software

There are a few different ways you can use the apt (Advanced Package Tool) package management system to find software and programs on a Linux system.

Searching for Packages by Name

You can use the search subcommand to search for a package by name. For example, to search for a package called package-name, you can use the following command:

```
apt-cache search package-name
```

This will search the package index for any packages that match the search term package-name and show you a list of the results.

Listing Installed Packages

To list all of the installed packages on your system, you can use the list subcommand with the --installed option:

```
apt list --installed
```

This will show you a list of all of the installed packages on your system, along with their versions and whether or not they are up-to-date.

Listing Available Packages

To list all of the packages that are available to be installed from the package repositories, you can use the list subcommand without any options:

```
apt list
```

This will show you a list of all of the packages that are available in the package repositories, along with their versions and whether or not they are already installed on your system.

It's worth noting that these are just a few examples of the many options and subcommands available with apt. You can find more information about using apt by consulting the apt-cache man page or the documentation for your specific Linux distribution.

Installing Software

On a Linux computer, you can use the install subcommand and then specify the name of the software package that you want to put in place by using the apt (Advanced Package Tool) package management system. This will allow you to install software and programs on your computer. For example, to install a package called package-name, you can use the following command:

```
sudo apt-get install package-name
```

This will download and install the package-name package, along with any dependencies that it requires.

You can also install multiple packages at the same time by specifying a list of package names separated by spaces:

```
sudo apt-get install package-name-1 package-name-2 package-
name-3
```

It's worth noting that you need to have root privileges (e.g., by using the sudo command) to be able to install software using apt.

It's also a good idea to update the package index files before installing a new package. You can do this by using the update subcommand:

```
sudo apt-get update
```

This will download the latest package index files from the package repositories and ensure that you have access to the most recent versions of all available packages.

It's worth noting that these are just a few examples of the many options and subcommands available with apt. You can find more information about using apt by consulting the apt-get man page or the documentation for your specific Linux distribution.

Removing Software

To remove software and programs using the apt (Advanced Package Tool) package management system on a Linux system, you can use the remove subcommand and specify the name of the package you want to remove. For example, to remove a package called package-name, you can use the following command:

```
sudo apt-get remove package-name
```

This will remove the package-name package, but it will leave the configuration files for the package behind.

To remove a package and its configuration files, you can use the purge subcommand:

```
sudo apt-get purge package-name
```

You can also remove multiple packages at the same time by specifying a list of package names separated by spaces:

```
sudo apt-get remove package-name-1 package-name-2 package-name-3
```

It's worth noting that you need to have root privileges (e.g., by using the sudo command) to be able to remove software using apt.

It's also a good idea to update the package index files before removing a package. You can do this by using the update subcommand:

```
sudo apt-get update
```

This will download the latest package index files from the package repositories and ensure that you have access to the most recent versions of all available packages.

Understanding Repositories

A repository is a central location where software packages are stored and made available for installation. Repositories are used by package management systems, such as apt or yum, to download and install software packages onto a Linux system.

Repositories can contain software packages for a wide range of purposes, including system libraries, applications, and utilities. The packages in a repository are typically organized into different categories and made available for different versions of a Linux distribution.

There are a few different types of repositories that are commonly used in Linux distributions:

- Official repositories - These are repositories that are maintained by the developers of a Linux distribution and contain software packages that are supported by the distribution.

- Third-party repositories - These are repositories that are maintained by organizations or individuals other than the developers of a Linux distribution and may contain software packages that are not included in the official repositories.

- Personal repositories - These are repositories that are created and maintained by individual users and may contain custom packages or packages that are not available in other repositories.

To use a repository with a package management system, you typically need to add the repository to the system's list of available repositories. This is typically done by adding a configuration file with the repository's details to the /etc/apt/sources.list.d/ directory (for apt) or by creating a new repository configuration file in the /etc/yum.repos.d/ directory (for yum).

Once a repository is added to the system, you can use the package management system to search for, install, update, and remove software packages from the repository.

Official Repositories

Official repositories are maintained by the developers of a Linux distribution and contain software packages that are supported by the distribution. These repositories typically contain a wide range of software packages, including system libraries, applications, and utilities, that are tested and packaged specifically for the distribution.

For example, Ubuntu has a set of official repositories that contain software packages for Ubuntu. These repositories include:

main - contains the majority of software packages that are supported by Ubuntu
restricted - contains software packages that are supported by Ubuntu but that may have legal or copyright restrictions
universe - contains software packages that are not officially supported by Ubuntu but that are maintained by the Ubuntu community
multiverse - contains software packages that are not officially supported by Ubuntu and that may have legal or copyright restrictions

Third-Party Repositories

Third-party repositories are maintained by organizations or individuals other than the developers of a Linux distribution and may contain software packages that are not included in the official repositories. These repositories may contain software packages that are not supported by the distribution, or that are not available in the official repositories for some other reason.

For example, Google maintains a third-party repository that contains software packages for Google Chrome and other Google-related applications. This repository can be added to a Debian or Ubuntu-based system to allow users to install these packages using apt.

Personal Repositories

Personal repositories are created and maintained by individual users and may contain custom packages or packages that are not available in other repositories. These repositories are typically used to share software packages with a small group of users, or to test packages before they are made available in a larger repository.

Personal repositories are usually hosted on a web server or file server and are added to a Linux system by adding a configuration file with the repository's details to the /etc/apt/sources.list.d/ directory (for apt) or by creating a new repository configuration file in the /etc/yum.repos.d/ directory (for yum).

It's worth noting that while using third-party or personal repositories can be convenient, it's important to be careful when adding these repositories to your system, as they may contain software packages that are not tested or supported by the distribution. It's a good idea to only use reputable repositories and to carefully review the packages that you install from these repositories.

Exploring 'sources.list' Files

Understanding 'source.list'

A sources.list file is a configuration file that contains a list of repositories that are available to a package management system, such as apt or yum. These files are used to specify the locations of the package repositories and allow the package management system to download and install software packages from these repositories.

On Debian and Ubuntu-based systems, the sources.list file is typically located in the /etc/apt/ directory and contains a list of repositories that are available to the apt package management system. The file is a plain text file and can be edited manually to add, remove, or modify the repositories that are included in the list.

The sources.list file has a specific format that consists of a repository type, a repository address, and a distribution codename. Following is an example of a sources.list file for a Debian-based system:

```
deb http://deb.debian.org/debian stable main
deb-src http://deb.debian.org/debian stable main

deb http://security.debian.org/ stable/updates main
deb-src http://security.debian.org/ stable/updates main
```

In this example, the file includes two repositories: the main Debian repository and the Debian security repository. The deb and deb-src lines specify the repository type (binary or source packages, respectively) and the repository address, while the stable and main parameters specify the distribution codename and the repository component, respectively.

It's worth noting that while the sources.list file is the main configuration file for the apt package management system, it is possible to add additional repositories to the system by creating separate configuration files in the /etc/apt/sources.list.d/ directory. These files have a .list extension and have the same format as the sources.list file.

View and Edit 'sources.list' File

To explore the sources.list file on a Debian or Ubuntu-based Linux system, you can use a text editor to open the file and view its contents. The sources.list file is a plain text file and can be edited using any text editor, such as nano, vi, or gedit.

Following is an example of how you might view the contents of the sources.list file using the nano text editor:

```
sudo nano /etc/apt/sources.list
```

This will open the sources.list file in the nano text editor and allow you to view and edit its contents.

The sources.list file has a specific format that consists of a repository type, a repository address, and a distribution codename. Following is an example of a sources.list file for a Debian-based system:

```
deb http://deb.debian.org/debian stable main
deb-src http://deb.debian.org/debian stable main

deb http://security.debian.org/ stable/updates main
deb-src http://security.debian.org/ stable/updates main
```

In this example, the file includes two repositories: the main Debian repository and the Debian security repository. The deb and deb-src lines specify the repository type (binary or source packages, respectively) and the repository address, while the stable and main parameters specify the distribution codename and the repository component, respectively.

You can view and edit the contents of the sources.list file using the nano text editor by moving the cursor using the arrow keys and making changes to the text. When you are finished, you can save your changes by pressing CTRL + O and exit the editor by pressing CTRL + X.

Hack#1: Managing Repositories

In Linux, package management systems such as apt, yum, and dnf use repositories to store and distribute software packages. You can use the "add-apt-repository" command to add new repositories to your system, for example:

```
sudo add-apt-repository ppa:webupd8team/sublime-text-3
```

This command will add the WebUpd8team's Sublime Text 3 repository to your system. You can also use the "apt-add-repository" command to add a repository that is not available in the default Ubuntu repositories.

Hack#2: Searching for Packages

To search for packages in Linux, you can use the package management system's built-in search function. For example, in Ubuntu you can use the following command to search for a package:

```
apt-cache search package_name
```

This will return a list of packages that match the search term you entered.

CHAPTER 5: ADMINISTERING OWNERSHIP AND PERMISSIONS

Overview of Commands

Ownership and permissions refer to the ability of users and processes to access and modify files and directories. Linux systems use a set of permission bits and ownership information to control access to files and directories.

There are a few different commands that you can use to view and modify ownership and permissions on a Kali Linux system. Following is a brief overview of some of the more common commands:

ls

The ls command is used to list the contents of a directory. You can use the -l option to show detailed information about each file and directory, including the ownership and permissions.

ls -l

This will show you a list of the files and directories in the current directory, along with information about the ownership and permissions for each item.

chown

The chown command is used to change the ownership of a file or directory. You can use the chown command to change the owner or group owner of a file or directory.

```
chown new-owner file

chown new-owner:new-group file
```

This will change the owner or group owner of the file to the specified new-owner or new-group, respectively.

chmod

The chmod command is used to change the permissions of a file or directory. You can use the chmod command to change the read permissions, write permissions, and execute permissions for a file or directory.

```
chmod octal-permissions file
```

This will change the permissions of the file to the specified octal permissions. Octal permissions are specified using a three-digit number, with each digit representing the read, write, and execute permissions for the owner, group, and other users, respectively.

For example, to give the owner read and write permissions, the group read permission, and no permissions to other users, you could use the following command:

```
chmod 640 file
```

You can also use symbolic permissions to specify the permissions using characters. For example, to give the owner read and write permissions, the group read permission, and no permissions to other users, you could use the following command:

```
chmod u+rw,g+r,o-rw file
```

Decimal Notation

Decimal notation is a way of representing numbers using the decimal (base 10) numeral system. Decimal notation is used in many different contexts in Linux, including when specifying permissions, file sizes, and other numeric values.

For example, when specifying file permissions in Linux, you can use decimal notation to represent the permission bits for a file. In decimal notation, each permission (e.g., read, write, execute) is represented by a specific number, and the permission bits for a file are represented by the sum of these numbers.

Using Decimal Notation

Following is an example of how the permission bits for a file might be represented in decimal notation:

```
rw-r--r-- - 644

rwxr-xr-x - 755

rwxrwxrwx - 777
```

In this example, the r permission is represented by the number 4, the w permission is represented by the number 2, and the x permission is represented by the number 1. The permission bits for a file are represented by the sum of these numbers for each permission (e.g., rw- is 6 because 4 + 2 = 6).

It's worth noting that while decimal notation is a common way of representing permission bits in Linux, you can also use octal notation (base 8) or symbolic notation to represent these permissions. You can find more information about representing permissions in Linux by consulting the documentation for your specific Linux distribution or by consulting online resources.

File Sizes

In Linux, file sizes are often represented in decimal notation using units of bytes, kilobytes, megabytes, gigabytes, etc. For example, a file that is 100KB in size might be represented as 100KB or 100,000 bytes.

File Timestamps

In Linux, file timestamps (e.g., the date and time that a file was last modified) are often represented in decimal notation as a Unix timestamp, which is the number of seconds that have elapsed since the start of the Unix epoch (midnight UTC on January 1, 1970).

For example, a file that was last modified on January 1, 2021 at 12:00 AM UTC might have a timestamp of 1609459200.

Network Addresses

In Linux, network addresses (e.g., IP addresses, MAC addresses) are often represented in decimal notation. For example, an IPv4 address might be represented as a series of four decimal numbers separated by dots (e.g., 192.168.1.1). Similarly, a MAC address might be represented as a series of six pairs of hexadecimal digits separated by colons (e.g., 00:11:22:33:44:55).

UGO

In Linux, UGO refers to the three basic types of users that can access a file or directory: the owner (U), the group (G), and other users (O). These terms are used to specify the permissions that are set for a file or directory, and they determine who is able to read, write, and execute the file or access the contents of the directory.

Permissions in Linux are specified using permission bits, which are a series of digits that represent the read, write, and execute permissions for the owner, group, and other users, respectively. Each permission is represented by a specific number, and the permission bits for a file or directory are represented by the sum of these numbers.

For example, the following table shows how the read, write, and execute permissions might be represented in decimal notation:

Permission	Decimal value
r	4
w	2
x	1

Specify Permission

To specify the permissions for a file or directory using UGO notation, you can use a combination of these values to represent the read, write, and execute permissions for the owner, group, and other users, respectively.

For example, to give the owner read, write, and execute permissions, the group read and execute permissions, and no permissions to other users, you could use the following command:

```
chmod u=rwx,g=rx,o= file
```

This command would set the permission bits for the file to 741, which represents read, write, and execute permissions for the owner (7), read and execute permissions for the group (4), and no permissions for other users (1).

It's worth noting that UGO notation is just one way of specifying permissions in Linux. You can also use octal notation or symbolic notation to specify permissions. For example, the same permissions as above could be specified using octal notation as follows:

```
chmod 741 file
```

Or using symbolic notation as follows:

```
chmod u+rwx,g+rx,o-rwx file
```

Masks

A mask is a value that is used to set or modify the permissions of a file or directory. Masks are typically used in conjunction with the umask command, which is used to set the default permissions for newly created files and directories.

The umask command takes a mask value as an argument, and this value is used to determine the default permissions that will be applied to newly created files and directories. The mask value is subtracted from the full permissions of rwxrwxrwx (777 in octal notation) to determine the default permissions.

‘umask’ Command

For example, if the mask value is 022, the default permissions for newly created files and directories will be 755 (rwxr-xr-x). If the mask value is 027, the default permissions will be 750 (rwxr-x---).

Following is an example of how you might use the umask command to set the default permissions for newly created files and directories:

```
umask 022
```

This command would set the mask value to 022 and cause newly created files and directories to have default permissions of 755 (rwxr-xr-x).

It's worth noting that the umask command only affects the default permissions for newly created files and directories. It does not modify the permissions of existing files or directories. To modify the permissions of existing files or directories, you can use the chmod command.

It's also worth noting that the mask value is typically specified in octal notation, with each digit representing the read, write, and execute permissions for the owner, group, and other users, respectively. For example, a mask value of 022 would represent read and write permissions for the owner, no permissions for the group, and read permissions for other users.

Here are a few more examples of mask values and their corresponding default permissions:

Mask value	Default permissions
022	rwxr-xr-x
027	rwxr-x---
007	rwx-------
077	rwx------

It's worth noting that the specific mask values and default permissions that are used on a Linux system may vary depending on the specific configuration and the needs of the users and processes on the system. You can find more information about specifying mask values and setting default permissions in Linux by consulting the documentation for your specific Linux distribution or by consulting online resources.

Display Current Mask Value

In addition to setting the default permissions for newly created files and directories, the umask command can also be used to display the current mask value. To display the current mask value, you can use the umask command with no arguments:

```
umask
```

This will display the current mask value in octal notation.

You can also use the umask command to set the mask value to a specific value. To do this, you can specify the desired mask value as an argument to the umask command. For example:

```
umask 022
```

This command would set the mask value to 022, which would cause newly created files and directories to have default permissions of 755 (rwxr-xr-x).

It's worth noting that the mask value that is set using the umask command is typically stored in a shell variable and is only effective for the current session. If you want to make the mask value persistent across sessions, you can set the mask value in the bashrc or profile configuration files, depending on your specific Linux distribution and shell.

Granting Ownership

Ownership refers to the user and group that own a file or directory. The owner of a file or directory has the ability to set permissions for the file or directory and to modify or delete the file or directory, depending on the permissions that are set.

To grant ownership of a file or directory in Linux, you can use the chown command. The chown command allows you to change the owner and group of a file or directory.

Following is an example of how you might use the chown command to grant ownership of a file to a different user:

```
chown new_owner file
```

This command would change the owner of the file to new_owner. You can also specify a group as the second argument to the chown command to change the group ownership of the file or directory.

To manage ownership of files and directories in Linux, you can use the chown command to change the owner and group of files and directories as needed. You can also use the chmod command to set permissions for files and directories, which can allow or restrict access to the files and directories by different users and groups.

It's worth noting that the chown and chmod commands are typically restricted to users with root privileges, so you may need to use the sudo command to execute these commands if you do not have root privileges. You can find more information about the chown and chmod commands and how to manage ownership and permissions in Linux by consulting the documentation for your specific Linux distribution or by consulting online resources.

Checking Permissions

Permissions refer to the ability of users and groups to access files and directories on the system. Permissions can be set to allow or restrict access to files and directories by different users and groups, and can be used to ensure that sensitive files and directories are protected from unauthorized access.

To check the permissions of a file or directory in Linux, you can use the ls -l command. The ls -l command displays a list of files and directories in a directory, along with their permissions and other attributes.

Following is an example of how you might use the ls -l command to check the permissions of a file:

```
ls -l file
```

This command would display the permissions of the file, along with the owner and group owner of the file and other information.

The permissions for a file or directory are displayed in the first field of the ls -l output. The permissions field is made up of 10 characters, with the first character indicating the file type (- for a regular file, d for a directory, etc.), and the next nine characters indicating the read, write, and execute permissions for the owner, group, and other users, respectively.

For example, the permissions rwxr-xr-x would indicate that the owner of the file has read, write, and execute permissions (rwx), the group owner has read and execute permissions (r-x), and other users have read and execute permissions (r-x).

Modifying Permissions

You can use the chmod command to modify the permissions of a file or directory. The chmod command allows you to change the read, write, and execute permissions for the owner, group, and other users for a file or directory.

There are two main ways to specify permissions when using the chmod command: the symbolic method and the octal method.

Symbolic Method

The symbolic method allows you to specify permissions using characters to represent the different permissions. The chmod command uses the following characters to represent permissions:

r: read permission
w: write permission
x: execute permission
-: no permission

To use the symbolic method, you can specify the permissions that you want to set for each user class (owner, group, and other users) as a combination of these characters. For example:

```
chmod u=rwx,g=rx,o=r file
```

This command would set read, write, and execute permissions for the owner (u) of the file, read and execute permissions for the group (g) owner of the file, and read permissions for other users (o).

Octal Method

The octal method allows you to specify permissions using a three-digit octal value. Each digit represents the permissions for a different user class (owner, group, and other users), with the following values:

0: no permission
1: execute permission
2: write permission
3: write and execute permissions
4: read permission
5: read and execute permissions
6: read and write permissions
7: read, write, and execute permissions

To use the octal method, you can specify the permissions that you want to set for each user class as a combination of these values. For example:

```
chmod 755 file
```

This command would set read, write, and execute permissions for the owner (7) of the file, read and execute permissions for the group (5) owner of the file, and read and execute permissions for other users (5).

Securing Permissions

Securing permissions in Linux involves setting appropriate permissions on files and directories to ensure that they are protected from unauthorized access. Properly securing permissions can help to protect sensitive data, prevent unauthorized changes to the system, and ensure that the system is stable and secure.

There are several ways that you can secure permissions in Linux, including:

- Setting restrictive permissions on sensitive files and directories: You can use the chmod command to set permissions on sensitive files and directories to restrict access to only authorized users.

- Setting the SUID and SGID bits appropriately: You can use the chmod command to set the SUID (Set User ID) and SGID (Set Group ID) bits on files and directories to allow specific users or groups to execute the files with higher privileges. However, it's important to use these bits with caution, as they can be a security risk if set on files or directories owned by untrusted or malicious users.

- Setting the sticky bit appropriately: You can use the chmod command to set the sticky bit on directories to prevent users from deleting or renaming files and directories within the directory unless they are the owner of the file or directory, the owner of the directory, or the root user. This can help to prevent accidental or malicious changes to files and directories within the directory.

- Setting appropriate permissions on system files and directories: You can use the chmod command to set restrictive permissions on system files and directories to prevent unauthorized access and changes.

To use the chmod command to secure permissions in Linux, you can specify the permissions that you want to set for each file or directory using either the symbolic method or the octal method. For example:

```
chmod u=rwx,g=,o= file
```

This command would set read, write, and execute permissions for the owner of the file and no permissions for the group owner and other users.

Root Permissions

The root user is the superuser, which means that it has complete control over the system. The root user has the ability to perform any action on the system, including modifying system files, installing and removing software, and creating and deleting users.

By default, the root user has full permissions to read, write, and execute all files and directories on the system, regardless of the permissions that are set for other users. This allows the root user to perform system-level tasks and make changes to the system that are not possible for regular users.

It's worth noting that the root user should be used with caution, as it has the ability to make changes to the system that could potentially cause instability or even render the system inoperable. As a result, it is generally recommended to log in as a regular user and use the sudo command to execute commands with root privileges only when necessary.

Manage Root Permissions

To manage root permissions in Linux, you can use the sudo command to execute commands with root privileges. The sudo command allows you to execute commands as the root user, but requires you to enter your own password to authenticate the command. This helps to prevent unauthorized access to root privileges and can help to prevent accidental or malicious changes to the system.

Following is an example of how you might use the sudo command to execute a command with root privileges:

```
sudo apt-get update
```

This command would update the package list for the apt package manager, which requires root privileges. When you execute this command, you will be prompted to enter your own password to authenticate the sudo command.

Special Permissions

Special permissions are a set of additional permission bits that can be set on files and directories to specify certain special behaviors or attributes. There are several different special permissions that can be set in Linux, including the SUID (Set User ID) and SGID (Set Group ID) bits, the sticky bit, and others.

Following is a brief overview of some of the more common special permissions in Linux:

SUID (Set User Id)

The SUID (Set User ID) permission is a special permission bit that can be set on a file or program. When the SUID bit is set on a file or program, it allows users to execute the file or program with the permissions of the owner of the file, rather than with the user's own permissions.

SGID (Set Group Id)

The SGID (Set Group ID) permission is similar to the SUID permission, but it applies to the group owner of the file rather than the user owner. When the SGID bit is set on a file or directory, it causes new files and directories created within the directory to inherit the group ownership of the directory, rather than the user's default group.

Sticky Bit

The sticky bit is a special permission bit that can be set on a directory. When the sticky bit is set on a directory, it prevents users from deleting or renaming files and directories within the directory unless they are the owner of the file or directory, the owner of the directory, or the root user.

t (Text) Bit

The t (text) bit is a special permission bit that is used to indicate that a file is a text file. When the t bit is set on a file, it tells certain programs (such as text editors) to treat the file as a text file, rather than as a binary

i (Immutable) Bit

The i (immutable) bit is a special permission bit that can be set on a file or directory. When the i bit is set on a file or directory, it prevents the file or directory from being modified or deleted, even by the root user. This can be useful for protecting important system files from accidental or malicious modification.

a (Append-Only) Bit

The a (append-only) bit is a special permission bit that can be set on a file. When the a bit is set on a file, it prevents the file from being modified or truncated, but allows new data to be appended to the end of the file. This can be useful for maintaining logs or other files that should not be modified, but should be allowed to grow over time.

d (No Dump) Bit

The d (no dump) bit is a special permission bit that can be set on a file or directory. When the d bit is set on a file or directory, it prevents the file or directory from being included in a dump or backup of the file system. This can be useful for excluding certain files or directories from backups or other system-level operations.

Hack#1: Preventing Accidental Changes

The sudo command allows you to execute commands with root privileges, which are the highest level of privileges on a Linux system. The root user has complete control over the system and has the ability to perform any action on the system, including modifying system files, installing and removing software, and creating and deleting users.

It's generally a good idea to log in as a regular user and use the sudo command to execute commands with root privileges only when necessary. This helps to prevent accidental or malicious changes to the system, as it requires you to authenticate the sudo command with your own password before it is executed.

Using the sudo command also helps to improve security, as it allows you to execute root commands without having to log in as the root user. This can help to prevent unauthorized access to root privileges and can help to prevent accidental or malicious changes to the system.

For example, if you need to update the package list for the apt package manager, you could use the following sudo command:

```
sudo apt-get update
```

This command would update the package list for the apt package manager, which requires root privileges. When you execute this command, you will be prompted to enter your own password to authenticate the sudo command.

Hack#2: Protecting Sensitive Files and Directories

To set restrictive permissions on sensitive files and directories using the chmod command in Linux, you can use either the symbolic method or the octal method to specify the permissions that you want to set.

Following is an example of how to set restrictive permissions on a sensitive file using the chmod command and the symbolic method:

```
sudo chmod u=rw,g=,o= /etc/shadow
```

This command would set read and write permissions for the owner of the /etc/shadow file and no permissions for the group owner and other users. The /etc/shadow file contains encrypted passwords for the system and is considered a sensitive file, so it's important to set restrictive permissions to prevent unauthorized access and changes.

Following is an example of how to set restrictive permissions on a sensitive directory using the chmod command and the octal method:

```
sudo chmod 700 /etc/ssh
```

This command would set read, write, and execute permissions for the owner of the /etc/ssh directory and no permissions for the group owner and other users. The /etc/ssh directory contains configuration files for the ssh service, which allows users to remotely connect to the system, and is considered a sensitive directory, so it's important to set restrictive permissions to prevent unauthorized access and changes.

Hack#3: Safely using SUID and SGID Bits

The SUID (Set User ID) and SGID (Set Group ID) bits in Linux allow you to set permissions on files and directories such that they are executed with the privileges of the owner or group owner, rather than the privileges of the user executing the file. This can be useful in certain situations, such as allowing users to execute certain commands with root privileges without logging in as the root user.

However, it's important to use the SUID and SGID bits with caution, as they can be a security risk if set on files or directories owned by untrusted or malicious users. If an attacker is able to gain control of a file or directory with SUID or SGID permissions, they may be able to execute the file with higher privileges and potentially compromise the system.

To safely use the SUID and SGID bits, you should only set them on files and directories that are owned by trusted users or groups and that need to be executed with higher privileges. You should also carefully review the permissions and ownership of files and directories with SUID and SGID permissions to ensure that they are not being used in an insecure manner.

Following is an example of how to safely use the SUID bit to allow users to execute the passwd command with root privileges:

```
sudo chmod 4755 /usr/bin/passwd
```

This command would set the SUID bit on the /usr/bin/passwd file, which allows users to change their own passwords. By setting the SUID bit on this file, users can execute the passwd command with root privileges without logging in as the root user.

CHAPTER 6: EXPLORING SHELLS: 'BASH', 'ZSH' AND 'FISH'

Understanding Shell

A shell is a command-line interface that allows you to interact with the operating system. It allows you to enter commands, run programs, and perform a wide range of tasks by typing commands at the command prompt.

Shell scripting is the process of writing scripts (sets of instructions) in a shell programming language to automate tasks or perform actions on a system. Shell scripts can be used to automate tasks, create and manage system configurations, and perform system maintenance and administration.

Shell scripting is popular among developers because it is a powerful and flexible way to automate tasks and perform actions on a system. It is also useful for developers who need to perform tasks or actions on multiple systems or in different environments, as shell scripts can be easily written and executed on a wide range of systems.

Shell scripting is also popular because it allows developers to take advantage of the many features and utilities provided by the shell, such as command line editing, command history, variables, and control structures. This can make it easier and more efficient to perform tasks and actions on a system.

There are several different shells available for Linux, each with its own set of features and capabilities. Three of the most popular shells for Linux are bash, zsh, and fish. Following is a brief overview of each of these shells:

bash

bash (Bourne-Again SHell) is the default shell on most Linux distributions. It is a command-line interface that allows you to interact with the operating system by entering commands at the command prompt. bash is a powerful and flexible shell that supports a wide range of features, including:

- Command line editing: bash allows you to edit and modify the command line using a variety of keystrokes and shortcuts.
- Command history: bash keeps a history of the commands that you have entered, which you can access using the history command or by using the up and down arrow keys.

- Variables: bash allows you to define and use variables to store data or information. You can use variables to store the output of a command, pass data between scripts, or set options and preferences.

- Control structures: bash supports a range of control structures, such as if statements, for loops, and while loops, which you can use to control the flow of execution in your scripts.

- Functions: bash allows you to define and use functions to organize and reuse code in your scripts.

- Wildcards: bash supports the use of wildcards, which you can use to specify a group of files or directories based on a pattern or expression.

- Piping and redirection: bash allows you to use the | (pipe) operator to send the output of one command to another command for further processing, and the > and < operators to redirect the input and output of a command to a file or another source.

bash is widely used and is a good choice for users who are familiar with the command line.

zsh

additional features such as improved command line editing, spelling correction, and support for plugins and themes.

Some of the key features of zsh include:

- Command line editing: zsh includes improved command line editing capabilities, such as automatic suggestions and correction of mistyped commands.

- Spelling correction: zsh includes a built-in spelling correction feature that suggests corrections for misspelled commands and arguments.

- Plugins and themes: zsh supports the use of plugins and themes, which allow you to extend the functionality of the shell and customize its appearance.

- Aliases: zsh allows you to define aliases for commands, which can be used to simplify or customize the way you interact with the shell.

- Functions: zsh supports the use of functions, which you can use to organize and reuse code in your scripts.

- Wildcards: zsh supports the use of wildcards, which you can use to specify a group of files or directories based on a pattern or expression.

- Auto-suggestions: zsh includes a built-in auto-suggestion feature that suggests possible commands and arguments as you type.

zsh is popular among advanced users and developers and is a good choice for users who want a more powerful and customizable shell.

fish

fish (Friendly Interactive SHell) is a user-friendly shell that is designed to be easy to use and understand. It is intended to be more intuitive and user-friendly than other shells, such as bash and zsh, and includes features such as syntax highlighting, auto-suggestions, and a built-in manual page viewer.

Some of the key features of fish include:

- Syntax highlighting: fish includes syntax highlighting, which highlights different elements of a command line (such as commands, arguments, and variables) in different colors to make it easier to read and understand.

- Auto-suggestions: fish includes a built-in auto-suggestion feature that suggests possible commands and arguments as you type.

- Manual page viewer: fish includes a built-in manual page viewer that allows you to view the documentation for commands and utilities without leaving the shell.

- Web-based configuration: fish allows you to configure the shell using a web-based interface, which can be more user-friendly and easier to use than other methods of configuration.

- Functions: fish supports the use of functions, which you can use to organize and reuse code in your scripts.

- Aliases: fish allows you to define aliases for commands, which can be used to simplify or customize the way you interact with the shell.

fish is a good choice for new users or users who want a more intuitive and user-friendly shell.

Popular Shell Commands

Following is a list of some popular universal shell commands that one can use with bash, fish and zsh:

- ls: Lists the files and directories in a directory.
- cd: Changes the current working directory.
- mkdir: Creates a new directory.
- rm: Deletes a file or directory.
- mv: Renames or moves a file or directory.
- cp: Copies a file or directory.
- cat: Displays the contents of a file.
- less: Displays the contents of a file one page at a time.
- grep: Searches for a pattern in a file or output.
- find: Searches for files and directories based on specified criteria.
- sort: Sorts the lines of a file or output.
- uniq: Removes duplicate lines from a file or output.
- wc: Counts the number of lines, words, and characters in a file or output.
- echo: Displays a message or the value of a variable.

- printf: Formats and displays a message or the value of a variable.
- chmod: Changes the permissions of a file or directory.
- chown: Changes the owner and group owner of a file or directory.

Creating First Bash Script

Steps to Write Bash Program

Writing a bash script is a simple process that involves creating a new text file and adding Bash commands to the file. Following is a step-by-step guide to writing your first bash script:

Open a text editor: To create a bash script, you will need to use a text editor to create a new file and enter your commands. You can use any text editor, such as vi, nano, or gedit, to create a bash script.

Add the #! shebang: The first line of your bash script should be #! followed by the path to the Bash interpreter. This tells the system which interpreter to use to execute the script. For example, you can use the following line to specify the Bash interpreter: #!/bin/bash.

Add your commands: After the shebang, you can add your Bash commands to the script. You can use any valid Bash commands, such as echo, cd, mkdir, or rm, to perform tasks or actions on the system.

Save the file: Save the file with a .sh file extension to indicate that it is a Bash script. For example, you could save the file as myscript.sh.

Make the script executable: To make the script executable, you will need to change its permissions using the chmod command. For example, you can use the following command to make the script executable: chmod +x myscript.sh.

Execute the script: To execute the script, you can use the ./ command followed by the name of the script. For example, you can use the following command to execute the script: ./myscript.sh.

Writing 'hello world' Program

Following is an example of a simple bash script that displays a message and lists the files in the current directory:

```
#!/bin/bash

echo "Hello, world!"
ls
```

This script will display the message "Hello, world!" and then list the files in the current directory when it is executed. You can find more information about writing and using bash scripts by consulting online resources or by consulting the documentation for your specific Linux distribution.

Writing Bash Program To Explore All Commands

Following is an example of a bash script that demonstrates some popular shell commands:

```
#!/bin/bash

# Display the current working directory
echo "Current working directory:"
pwd

# List the files and directories in the current directory
echo "Files and directories in the current directory:"
ls

# Create a new directory
echo "Creating a new directory..."
mkdir newdir
```

```
# Change to the new directory
echo "Changing to the new directory..."
cd newdir

# Display the current working directory
echo "Current working directory:"
pwd

# Copy a file from the parent directory
echo "Copying a file from the parent directory..."
cp ../file.txt .

# Display the contents of the file
echo "Contents of the file:"
cat file.txt

# Go back to the parent directory
echo "Going back to the parent directory..."
cd ..

# Delete the new directory and its contents
echo "Deleting the new directory and its contents..."
rm -rf newdir
```

This script demonstrates how to use commands such as pwd, ls, mkdir, cd, cp, cat, and rm to perform tasks and actions on a system. You can find more information about these and other popular shell commands by consulting online resources or by consulting the documentation for your specific shell.

Here is the output of the previous bash script:

```
Current working directory:
/home/user
Files and directories in the current directory:
file1.txt file2.txt dir1 dir2
Creating a new directory...
Changing to the new directory...
Current working directory:
/home/user/newdir
Copying a file from the parent directory...
Contents of the file:
This is the contents of the file.
Going back to the parent directory...
Deleting the new directory and its contents...
```

This output shows the results of the various commands that are executed in the script, including the current working directory, the files and directories in the current directory, and the contents of the copied file. You can modify the script to perform different tasks or actions and see how the output changes.

Using Arithmetic Expressions

Understanding Expressions

Arithmetic expressions in shell allow you to perform arithmetic operations, such as addition, subtraction, multiplication, and division, within a shell script or on the command line. In Bash, you can use the $((...)) syntax to evaluate an arithmetic expression and assign its value to a variable or display it on the command line.

Sample Program to Perform Arithmetic Operations

Following is an example of using arithmetic expressions in Bash:

```
# Perform arithmetic operations
a=10
b=5
c=$((a + b))
echo "a + b = $c"
c=$((a - b))
echo "a - b = $c"
c=$((a * b))
echo "a * b = $c"
c=$((a / b))
echo "a / b = $c"
```

This script demonstrates how to use the $((...)) syntax to perform arithmetic operations and assign the results to a variable. The output of this script will be:

```
a + b = 15
a - b = 5
```

```
a * b = 50
a / b = 2
```

Using 'if' Expressions

Understanding 'if' Syntax

If expressions in shell allow you to execute a block of code only if a specific condition is true. In Bash, you can use the if keyword to create an if expression and specify a condition using a test expression. If the test expression evaluates to true, the code in the if block will be executed.

Here is the basic syntax for an if expression in Bash:

```
if test-expression
then
    # code to be executed if test-expression is true
fi
```

Sample Program to Use 'if'

Following is an example of using an if expression in Bash:

```
# Prompt the user for a number
read -p "Enter a number: " number

# Check if the number is greater than 10
if [[ $number -gt 10 ]]
then
```

```
    echo "The number is greater than 10."
fi
```

This script prompts the user for a number and then checks if the number is greater than 10 using the -gt operator. If the number is greater than 10, the message "The number is greater than 10." will be displayed.

Using 'else' Expressions

Understanding 'else' Syntax

The else keyword in Bash is used in conjunction with an if expression to specify a block of code to be executed if the test expression in the if statement evaluates to false. Here is the basic syntax for using an else statement in Bash:

```
if test-expression
then
    # code to be executed if test-expression is true
else
    # code to be executed if test-expression is false
fi
```

Sample Program to Use 'else'

Following is an example of a Bash script that uses an else statement:

```
# Prompt the user for a number
read -p "Enter a number: " number
```

```
# Check if the number is even or odd
if [[ $((number % 2)) -eq 0 ]]
then
    echo "The number is even."
else
    echo "The number is odd."
fi
```

This script prompts the user for a number and then uses the % operator to check if the number is even or odd. If the number is even, the message "The number is even." will be displayed. If the number is odd, the message "The number is odd." will be displayed.

Using For Loops

Understanding 'for' Syntax

For loops in Bash allow you to execute a block of code repeatedly for a specified number of times or for each item in a list. Here is the basic syntax for a for loop in Bash:

```
for variable in list
do
    # code to be executed for each item in the list
done
```

Sample Program to Use 'for'

Following is an example of a Bash script that uses a for loop:

```
# Display the numbers 1 to 10
for i in {1..10}
do
    echo "$i"
done
```

This script uses a for loop to display the numbers 1 to 10. The for loop iterates over the range {1..10} and assigns each value in the range to the variable i. The code in the loop body, echo "$i", is then executed for each value of i. The output of this script will be:

```
1
2
3
4
5
6
7
8
9
10
```

Using While Loops

Understanding 'while' Loops

A while loop in Linux is a type of loop that repeatedly executes a block of commands as long as a certain condition is true. The basic syntax of a while loop is:

```
while [condition]; do
    [commands]
done
```

The condition is specified after the while keyword and is enclosed in square brackets []. If the condition is true, the commands inside the do and done keywords will be executed, and the loop will continue. If the condition is false, the loop will exit and the program will continue with the next instruction.

Sample Program to Use 'while' Loops

Following is an example of a while loop that counts from 1 to 10:

```
#!/bin/bash
count=1

while [ $count -le 10 ]; do
    echo $count
    count=$((count+1))
done
```

This script will output the numbers from 1 to 10, incrementing the count variable each iteration.

The output of the script will be as follows:

```
1
2
3
```

```
4
5
6
7
8
9
10
```

As you can see, the script starts by initializing a variable called count with the value of 1. Then, the while loop starts and the condition [$count -le 10] is evaluated. Since the value of count is 1 and 1 is less than or equal to 10, the commands inside the loop are executed. The first command inside the loop is echo $count, which prints the current value of count to the terminal. The second command is count=$((count+1)), which increments the value of count by 1.

After the commands inside the loop are executed, the loop goes back to the beginning and the condition is evaluated again. This process continues until the value of count becomes greater than 10, at which point the loop exits and the program continues with the next instruction.

Using Functions

What are Functions?

Functions in Linux are a way to group a set of commands together and give them a name. This allows you to reuse the commands multiple times without having to type them out again. Functions are defined using the function keyword, followed by the function name and a set of commands enclosed in curly braces {}. The basic syntax of a function is:

```
function function_name {
    [commands]
}
```

Functions can also be defined using the keyword function_name () which is a POSIX compliant way of defining a function.

```
function_name () {
    [commands]
}
```

Here's an example of a function that prints "Hello, World!" to the terminal:

```
#!/bin/bash

hello() {
    echo "Hello, World!"
}

hello
```

In this example, the function hello is defined with a single command echo "Hello, World!". The function is then called on the last line of the script by simply typing its name and executing it.

Functions can also take arguments and return values. Arguments passed to a function are specified within the parentheses following the function name, and are accessed inside the function using the $1, $2, etc. variables. Functions can also return a value using the return command, which sets the exit status of the function.

Functions are useful for organizing and structuring code, and for modularizing complex scripts. They also make it easy to reuse code and make it more readable and maintainable.

Sample Progrm to Use Functions

Following is an example of a bash script that defines a function and then calls it to execute a command:

```
#!/bin/bash

# Define the function
function hello {
    echo "Hello, World!"
}

# Call the function
hello

# Define a function that takes an argument
function greet {
    echo "Hello, $1!"
}

# Call the function and pass an argument
greet "John"

# Define a function that returns a value
function add {
    return $(( $1 + $2 ))
}

# Call the function and store the returned value
```

```
add 2 3
result=$?
echo "The result is $result"
```

In this example, the first function hello is defined with a single command echo "Hello, World!" . The function is then called on the script by typing its name and executing it. The second function greet takes an argument and uses it in the echo command. The third function add takes two arguments, performs an arithmetic operation on them and returns the result using the return command. The value returned by the function is stored in the $? variable, which is used to print the result of the operation.

Hack#1: Use of Command Line Options

Use command line options: Many Linux commands have a variety of options that can be used to modify their behavior. For example, the ls command has the -l option, which displays the files in a long format, showing the permissions, ownership, size, and timestamp of each file. Following is an example:

```
ls -l /usr/local
```

This command lists the files in the /usr/local directory in a long format.

Hack#2: Use of Shell Variables

Use shell variables: Shell variables are a powerful way to store and manipulate data in your scripts. Here's an example of how to use a variable in a shell script:

```
#!/bin/bash

name="John"
echo "Hello, $name"
```

In this example, the variable name is assigned the value "John" and is used in the echo command to print a personalized greeting.

Hack#3: Use of && Operator

Use the && operator: The && operator allows you to chain commands together and execute them only if the previous command succeeded. Here's an example:

```
#!/bin/bash

touch file.txt && echo "File created successfully"
```

In this example, the touch command is used to create a new file called "file.txt", and the echo command is used to display a message if the file was created successfully. If the touch command fails to create the file, the echo command would not be executed.

Hack#4: Use of || Operator

Use the || operator: The || operator allows you to chain commands together and execute them only if the previous command failed. Here's an example:

```
#!/bin/bash

touch file.txt || echo "File creation failed"
```

In this example, the touch command is used to create a new file called "file.txt", and the echo command is used to display a message if the file creation fails. If the touch command successfully creates the file, the echo command would not be executed.

Hack#5: Use of Shift Command

The shift command is a useful tool for working with positional parameters in shell scripts. Here's an example:

```
#!/bin/bash

while [ $# -gt 0 ]; do
    echo $1
    shift
done
```

In this example, a while loop is used to iterate through the positional parameters and print each one to the screen. The shift command is used inside the loop to shift the positional parameters to the left by one position, effectively removing the first parameter from the list and moving the others to the left.

CHAPTER 7: STORAGE MANAGEMENT

Overview of Storage Commands

Introduction

Storage commands are command-line utilities that are used to manage and manipulate storage devices and file systems in a Linux operating system. These commands can be used to perform a wide range of tasks, including:

- Displaying information about storage devices and file systems: Commands like df, du, lsblk, and fdisk can be used to view information about the amount of available and used disk space, partitions, and file systems.

- Formatting and partitioning storage devices: Commands like fdisk and mkfs can be used to format and partition storage devices, such as hard drives and USB drives, making them ready for use.

- Mounting and unmounting file systems: The mount and umount commands can be used to make a file system available for use (mount) or unavailable for use (unmount).

- Creating, managing and deleting logical volume: lvcreate, lvdisplay and lvremove commands can be used to create, manage and delete logical volumes.

- Checking and repairing file system errors: The fsck command can be used to check and repair file system errors, ensuring that the file system is in a consistent state.

Benefits of Storage Commands

- They are simple and efficient way to manage storage and file systems on a Linux machine
- Provides granular control over storage devices and file systems
- Automation of storage management tasks
- Help to perform storage management tasks remotely

Applications of Storage Commands:

- Disk management and maintenance
- Backups and recovery

- Partitioning and formatting of storage devices
- Mounting and unmounting file systems
- Managing and monitoring disk usage
- Logical volume management
- File system checking and repairing
- Remote storage management

List of Popular Commands

There are many storage-related commands used in Linux that can be useful for both hackers and administrators. Some of the most popular include:

- df: This command displays the amount of disk space used and available on all mounted file systems.

- du: This command shows the amount of disk space used by each file and directory in a file system.

- lsblk: This command lists information about all available block devices, including disk partitions and storage devices.

- fdisk: This command is used to partition and format storage devices, such as hard drives and USB drives.

- mount: This command mounts a file system, making it available for use.

- umount: This command unmounts a file system, making it unavailable for use.

- lvcreate: This command creates a logical volume on a Linux machine

- lvdisplay: This command displays information about logical volumes

- lvremove: This command deletes a logical volume.

- mkfs: This command creates a file system on a storage device, such as ext2, ext3, ext4, xfs, and others.

- fsck: This command checks and repairs file system errors.

Overall, these storage commands are extremely powerful and versatile tools that can be used to perform a wide range of storage management tasks on a Linux system.

Detecting Storage Drives

Detection of storage devices and file systems in Linux can be done by using a variety of commands and tools. Some of the most commonly used commands for this task include:

Using 'lsblk'

This command is used to list information about all available block devices, including disk partitions and storage devices. It can be used to display the device name, size, type, and mount point of each storage device. For example, to list all block devices on the system, you can use the command:

```
lsblk
```

The output of the above command might look like this:

```
NAME    MAJ:MIN RM   SIZE RO TYPE MOUNTPOINT
sda       8:0    0   1.8T  0 disk
├─sda1    8:1    0   512M  0 part /boot/efi
├─sda2    8:2    0   500M  0 part /boot
└─sda3    8:3    0   1.8T  0 part
  ├─vg_data-lv_root (dm-0) 253:0    0    100G  0 lvm  /
  ├─vg_data-lv_swap (dm-1) 253:1    0    16G   0 lvm  [SWAP]
  ├─vg_data-lv_home (dm-2) 253:2    0    1.7T  0 lvm  /home
```

Using 'fdisk'

This command is used to display information about disk partitions and storage devices. It can be used to display the device name, size, type, and partition table of each storage device. For example, to list all partitions on a specific device, you can use the command:

```
fdisk -l /dev/sdX
```

the output of the above command might look like this:

```
Disk /dev/sda: 1.8 TiB, 2000398934016 bytes, 3907029168
sectors
Units: sectors of 1 * 512 = 512 bytes
Sector size (logical/physical): 512 bytes / 4096 bytes
I/O size (minimum/optimal): 4096 bytes / 4096 bytes
Disklabel type: gpt
Disk identifier: xxxxxxxx-xxxx-xxxx-xxxx-xxxxxxxxxxxx

Device      Start        End    Sectors   Size Type
/dev/sda1      2048    1050623    1048576   512M EFI System
/dev/sda2   1050624    1550335      499712    244M Linux
filesystem
/dev/sda3    1550336 3907028991 3905478656      1.8T Linux
filesystem
```

Using 'dmesg'

This command is used to display kernel message log. This command can be useful to detect new storage device that has been added to the system after boot. The command will display all the information related to the storage devices, including the name, size, and type. For example, to check the kernel message log for new storage devices, you can use the command:

```
dmesg | grep -i "sd"
```

the output of the above command might look like this:

```
[    1.278396] sd 0:0:0:0: [sda] 3907029168 512-byte logical
blocks: (2.00 TB/1.82 TiB)
[    1.278407] sd 0:0:0:0: [sda] 4096-byte physical blocks
[    1.278489] sd 0:0:0:0: [sda] Write Protect is off
[    1.278493] sd 0:0:0:0: [sda] Mode Sense: 00 3a 00 00
[    1.278638] sd 0:0:0:0: [sda] Write cache: enabled, read
cache: enabled, doesn't support DPO or FUA
```

Using 'parted'

This command is used to display the partition table of a storage device. It can be used to display the device name, size, type, and partition table of each storage device. For example, to list the partition table of a specific device, you can use the command:

```
parted /dev/sdX print
```

the output of the above command might look like this:

```
Model: ATA WDC WD20EZRZ-00Z (scsi)
Disk /dev/sda: 2000GB
Sector size (logical/physical): 512B/4096B
```

```
Partition Table: gpt
Disk Flags:

Number Start End Size File system Name Flags
1 1049kB 538MB 537MB fat32 boot esp
2 538MB 781MB 244MB ext2 boot
3 781MB 2000GB 1999GB ext4 primary
```

Using 'blkid'

This command is used to display information about all available block devices, including disk partitions and storage devices. It can be used to display the device name, UUID, label, type, and mount point of each storage device. For example, to list all block devices on the system, you can use the command:

```
blkid
```

the output of the above command might look like this:

```
/dev/sda1: UUID="xxxxxxxx-xxxx-xxxx-xxxx-xxxxxxxxxxxx"
TYPE="vfat" PARTUUID="xxxxxxxx-xxxx-xxxx-xxxx-xxxxxxxxxxxx"
/dev/sda2: UUID="xxxxxxxx-xxxx-xxxx-xxxx-xxxxxxxxxxxx"
TYPE="ext2" PARTUUID="xxxxxxxx-xxxx-xxxx-xxxx-xxxxxxxxxxxx"
/dev/sda3: UUID="xxxxxxxx-xxxx-xxxx-xxxx-xxxxxxxxxxxx"
TYPE="ext4" PARTUUID="xxxxxxxx-xxxx-xxxx-xxxx-xxxxxxxxxxxx"
/dev/mapper/vg_data-lv_root: UUID="xxxxxxxx-xxxx-xxxx-xxxx-
xxxxxxxxxxxx" TYPE="ext4"
```

```
/dev/mapper/vg_data-lv_swap:  UUID="xxxxxxxx-xxxx-xxxx-xxxx-xxxxxxxxxxxx" TYPE="swap"
/dev/mapper/vg_data-lv_home:  UUID="xxxxxxxx-xxxx-xxxx-xxxx-xxxxxxxxxxxx" TYPE="ext4"
```

Using '/proc/mounts'

It is a virtual file that contains information about all mounted file systems. The file contains the file system type, mount point, and device name. For example, to check the mounted file systems, you can use the command:

```
cat /proc/mounts
```

the output of the above command might look like this:

```
/dev/sda1 /boot/efi vfat rw,relatime,fmask=0022,dmask=0022,codepage=437,iocharset=iso8859-1,shortname=mixed,errors=remount-ro 0 0
/dev/sda2 /boot ext2 rw,relatime,errors=remount-ro 0 0
/dev/mapper/vg_data-lv_root / ext4 rw,relatime,errors=remount-ro 0 0
/dev/mapper/vg_data-lv_home /home ext4 rw,relatime 0 0
```

Disk Partitioning

Understanding Partition Tables, Types and Mount Points

Disk partitioning in Linux is the process of dividing a storage device, such as a hard drive or SSD, into multiple logical units called partitions. Each partition can be formatted with a different file system and can be mounted to a different location in the file system hierarchy.

Here are some essential concepts related to disk partitioning in Linux:

Partition table: A partition table is a data structure that is used to store information about the partitions on a storage device. The most common partition table formats in Linux are Master Boot Record (MBR) and GUID Partition Table (GPT). MBR is limited to a maximum of four primary partitions, or three primary partitions and one extended partition. GPT, on the other hand, allows for a much larger number of partitions and also includes a backup copy of the partition table for added reliability.

Partition types: Each partition on a storage device can be assigned a specific partition type, which can be used to indicate the intended use of the partition. Some common partition types include primary, extended, and logical partitions.

File systems: A file system is a way of organizing and storing files on a storage device. Some common file systems used in Linux include ext2, ext3, ext4, xfs, btrfs, and others.

Mount points: A mount point is a location in the file system hierarchy where a partition is mounted and made available for use. For example, the root partition is typically mounted at /, and a home partition is typically mounted at /home.

Create New Partitions

For example, to create a new partition on /dev/sda, you can use the command:

```
sudo fdisk /dev/sda
```

This will open the fdisk prompt, where you can use various commands to manage partitions.

```
Command (m for help): n
Partition type
   p   primary (0 primary, 0 extended, 4 free)
   e   extended (container for logical partitions)
```

```
Select (default p): p
Partition number (1-4, default 1): 1
First sector (2048-3907029167, default 2048):
Last sector, +sectors or +size{K,M,G,T,P} (2048-3907029167,
default 3907029167): +100G

Command (m for help): w
The partition table has been altered.
Calling ioctl() to re-read partition table.
Syncing disks.
```

The above command created a primary partition with 100GB size on the /dev/sda disk

Modify Partitions

Parted command is similar to fdisk and can also be used to create, delete, and modify partitions on a storage device. For example, to create a partition on /dev/sda with a size of 100GB, you can use the command:

```
sudo parted /dev/sda mkpart primary ext4 0 100G
```

Mount Partitions

mount command is used to mount a partition and make it available for use. For example, to mount /dev/sda1 at /mnt, you can use the command:

```
sudo mount /dev/sda1 /mnt
```

Unmount Partitions

umount: This command is used to unmount a partition and make it unavailable for use. For example, to unmount the partition mounted at /mnt, you can use the command:

```
sudo umount /mnt
```

It's important to note that disk partitioning is a sensitive task because it involves modifying the structure of a storage device, which can have serious consequences if not done properly.

Here are some reasons why disk partitioning is considered a sensitive task:

- Data loss: If partitions are created, deleted, or modified incorrectly, it can result in the loss of data on the storage device. This can happen if a partition is accidentally deleted, or if a new partition is created over an existing one.
- File system corruption: If a file system is created or modified incorrectly, it can become corrupted and cause data loss or make the storage device inaccessible.
- Boot failure: If the partition table or bootloader is modified incorrectly, it can cause the system to fail to boot.
- Disk failure: In some cases, disk partitioning can cause physical damage to the storage device, resulting in complete data loss or the inability to use the device at all.

That's why it's important to have a backup of data before partitioning, also it's important to be very careful when using partitioning commands and to understand how they work before using them. Additionally, it's a good practice to test the partitioning process on a non-critical system before applying it to a production system.

Working Around Filesystems

A filesystem in Linux is a way of organizing and storing files on a storage device, such as a hard drive or SSD. It is responsible for managing the structure of the files, directories and metadata on a storage device. Some common file systems used in Linux include ext2, ext3, ext4, xfs, btrfs, and others. Each file system has its own features, advantages, and disadvantages, and different file systems are more suitable for different use cases.

Tasks around filesystems for hackers include:

- File system analysis: A hacker may analyze a file system to identify sensitive files, hidden directories, and other information that can be used to gain unauthorized access or steal data.

- File system enumeration: A hacker may use various commands and tools to enumerate the contents of a file system, such as listing all files and directories, and identifying file permissions and ownership.
- File system manipulation: A hacker may use various commands and tools to manipulate the contents of a file system, such as creating, deleting, or modifying files and directories, and changing file permissions and ownership.

- File system mounting: A hacker may use various commands and tools to mount a file system, such as in the case of forensic analysis, or to access files on a file system that is not normally accessible.

- File system encryption: A hacker may use various tools to encrypt a file system, such as LUKS, to protect the files from unauthorized access.

- File system forensics: A hacker may use various tools and techniques to perform forensic analysis of a file system, such as recovering deleted files, identifying file system artifacts, and analyzing file system metadata.

Create Filesystem

Mkfs command is used to create a file system on a partition. For example, to create an ext4 file system on /dev/sda1, you can use the command:

```
sudo mkfs.ext4 /dev/sda1
```

This command will create an ext4 file system on /dev/sda1 partition, for example:

```
mke2fs 1.45.5 (07-Jan-2020)
```

```
Creating filesystem with 26214400 4k blocks and 6553600
inodes
Filesystem UUID: xxxxxxxx-xxxx-xxxx-xxxx-xxxxxxxxxxxx
Superblock backups stored on blocks:
    32768, 98304, 163840, 229376, 294912, 819200, 884736,
1605632, 2654208,
    4096000, 7962624, 11239424, 20480000

Allocating group tables: done
Writing inode tables: done
Creating journal (16384 blocks): done
Writing superblocks and filesystem accounting information:
done
```

Resize Filesystem

resize2fs command is used to resize ext2, ext3, or ext4 file systems. For example, to resize a ext4 partition /dev/sda1 to 100GB, you can use the command:

```
sudo resize2fs /dev/sda1 100G
```

This command will resize the /dev/sda1 partition to 100GB , for example:

```
resize2fs 1.45.5 (07-Jan-2020)
Resizing the filesystem on /dev/sda1 to 262144000 (4k)
blocks.
The filesystem on /dev/sda1 is now 262144000 (4k) blocks long.
```

Encrypting Filesystem

Encrypting a filesystem in Linux typically involves creating an encrypted container using a tool like LUKS (Linux Unified Key Setup) and then formatting the container with a filesystem like ext4. Following is a sample application that demonstrates the process of encrypting a filesystem using LUKS:

```
# Create an encrypted container on /dev/sda1
sudo cryptsetup luksFormat /dev/sda1

# Open the container and assign it a name (e.g. "mycontainer")
sudo cryptsetup luksOpen /dev/sda1 mycontainer

# Format the container with ext4 filesystem
sudo mkfs.ext4 /dev/mapper/mycontainer

# Create a mount point (e.g. /mnt/encrypted)
sudo mkdir /mnt/encrypted

# Mount the container
sudo mount /dev/mapper/mycontainer /mnt/encrypted

# (Optional) Add an entry to /etc/fstab to mount the container
automatically at boot
echo '/dev/mapper/mycontainer /mnt/encrypted ext4 defaults 0
0' | sudo tee -a /etc/fstab
```

This sample application creates an encrypted container on the /dev/sda1 device and then formats it with an ext4 filesystem, and then mounts it at /mnt/encrypted.

It's important to note that encrypting a filesystem will protect the data stored on the filesystem from unauthorized access but it will not protect the data stored on the filesystem from malware or other malicious software that may already be running on the system.

It's also important to note that once you encrypt a filesystem you must remember the passphrase used to encrypt the filesystem, or else you will not be able to access the data stored on the filesystem.

Identifying Hidden Directory

A hidden directory is a directory whose name starts with a dot (.). These directories are not shown by default when listing the contents of a directory with the ls command, but they can still be accessed and manipulated like any other directory.

Following is a sample application that demonstrates how to identify a hidden directory:

```
# Change the current directory to /home
cd /home

# Use the -a option to show hidden files and directories with
ls command
ls -a
```

This will list all the files and directories in the /home directory, including hidden directories.

Another way to identify hidden directory is using the command find

```
# Find all hidden directories in /home
find /home -type d -name ".*"
```

This will search for all directories in /home whose names start with a dot.

You can also use the command ls -la to list all files and directories including hidden ones with their details, this way you can quickly identify hidden directories.

It's worth noting that these commands will only identify hidden directories that are in the directory where you're running the command from and its subdirectories, it does not search the entire file system.

Hidden directories can be used to store sensitive information, such as configuration files and credentials. Hackers can use these directories to hide malicious files and directories and evade detection.

Detecting Filesystem Errors

Types of Filesystem Errors

There are several types of filesystem errors that can occur in Linux, some of which include:

- File system corruption: This occurs when the file system's structure becomes damaged or inconsistent. This can happen due to a variety of reasons, such as a power failure, a software bug, or a hardware failure. Symptoms of file system corruption can include:
    - Inability to mount the file system
    - Inability to access files on the file system
    - Error messages when trying to access files on the file system
    - Data loss

- Disk space errors: This occurs when the file system runs out of disk space, which can cause the system to become unstable, or prevent new files from being created. Symptoms of disk space errors can include:
    - Error messages when trying to create new files
    - Programs or services becoming unresponsive
    - Inability to save files or complete tasks

- Inode errors: This occurs when the file system's inode table becomes corrupted or inconsistent. Inodes are data structures that store information about files and directories, such as ownership, permissions, and timestamps. Symptoms of inode errors can include:
    - Error messages when trying to access files or directories
    - Data loss
    - Files or directories becoming inaccessible

- Permission errors: This occurs when files or directories are set with incorrect permissions, which can prevent users or programs from accessing them. Symptoms of permission errors can include:
    - Error messages when trying to access files or directories
    - Programs or services becoming unresponsive

- Journaling errors: Journaling file systems keep a journal of file system operations to quickly recover the file system after a crash or unclean shutdown. This type of errors occur when the journal becomes corrupted, resulting in data loss or file system corruption.

- Bad blocks errors: This type of errors occur when a disk has physical bad blocks or sectors that can't be accessed. This can cause data loss or file system corruption.

It's important to note that these errors can be caused by a variety of factors, such as hardware failure, software bugs, or human error. They can also be caused by malware, viruses, or other malicious software.

There are several commands and tools that can be used to detect filesystem errors in Linux. Here are a few examples of applications that can be used to detect such errors:

Using 'fsck'

This command is used to check and repair file systems. It can be used to detect and repair errors in file systems such as ext2, ext3, and ext4. For example, to check the file system on /dev/sda1, you can use the command:

```
sudo fsck /dev/sda1
```

When you run the command sudo fsck /dev/sda1, it will check the file system and display any errors it finds. The output may look like this:

```
fsck from util-linux 2.34
e2fsck 1.45.5 (07-Jan-2020)
/dev/sda1 contains a file system with errors, check forced.
Pass 1: Checking inodes, blocks, and sizes
Pass 2: Checking directory structure
Pass 3: Checking directory connectivity
Pass 4: Checking reference counts
Pass 5: Checking group summary information
/dev/sda1: ***** FILE SYSTEM WAS MODIFIED *****
/dev/sda1: ********** WARNING: Filesystem still has errors
**********
```

This output indicates that there are errors on the file system and it's modified it.

Using 'dumpe2fs'

This command is used to display information about an ext2, ext3, or ext4 file system. It can be used to detect errors and inconsistencies in the file system. For example, to display information about the file system on /dev/sda1, you can use the command:

```
sudo dumpe2fs /dev/sda1
```

when you run the command sudo dumpe2fs /dev/sda1, it will display information about the file system. The output may look like this:

```
dumpe2fs 1.45.5 (07-Jan-2020)
Filesystem volume name:   <none>
Last mounted on:          <not available>
```

```
Filesystem   UUID:                    b7b2a1c8-d9d6-4b7c-a1f8-
7a8c6b9a7a9d
Filesystem magic number:  0xEF53
Filesystem revision #:    1 (dynamic)
Filesystem features:       has_journal ext_attr resize_inode
dir_index  filetype  extent  64bit  flex_bg  sparse_super
large_file
Filesystem flags:         signed_directory_hash
Default mount
options: (none)
Filesystem state: clean
Errors behavior: Continue
Filesystem OS type: Linux
Inode count: 262144
Block count: 1048576
Reserved block count: 52428
Free blocks: 950818
Free inodes: 261858
First block: 0
Block size: 4096
Fragment size: 4096
Reserved GDT blocks: 993
Blocks per group: 8192
```

```
Fragments per group: 8192
Inodes per group: 2048
Inode blocks per group: 256
Flex block group size: 16
Filesystem created: Mon Jan 4 14:35:46 2021
Last mount time: Mon Jan 4 14:35:46 2021
Last write time: Mon Jan 4 14:35:46 2021
Mount count: 0
Maximum mount count: -1
Last checked: Mon Jan 4 14:35:46 2021
Check interval: 0 (<none>)
Lifetime writes: 0
Reserved blocks uid: 0 (user root)
Reserved blocks gid: 0 (group root)
First inode: 11
Inode size: 256
Required extra isize: 28
Desired extra isize: 28
Journal inode: 8
First orphan inode: 0
Default directory hash: half_md4
Directory Hash Seed: 8d8c8b8a-8987-86e5-b3c2-a19f8e8d8c8b
Journal backup: inode blocks
```

This output provides detailed information about the file system, including the UUID, block size, inode count, and other parameters.

Using 'badblocks'

This command is used to search for bad blocks on a storage device. It can be used to detect errors caused by bad sectors on a disk. For example, to check for bad blocks on /dev/sda, you can use the command:

```
sudo badblocks -sv /dev/sda
```

when you run the command `sudo badblocks -sv /dev/sda`, it will search for bad blocks on the device and display the status of each block, number of bad blocks and the block number. The output may look like this:

```
Checking blocks 0 to 976773166
Checking for bad blocks (non-destructive read-write test)
Testing with random pattern: done
Pass completed, 0 bad blocks found. (0/0/0 errors)
```

This output indicates that no bad blocks were found on the device.

Using 'smartctl'

This command is used to display information about the status of storage devices. It can be used to detect errors in storage devices, such as hard drives, SSDs, and RAID arrays. For example, to display information about the status of /dev/sda, you can use the command:

```
sudo smartctl -a /dev/sda
```

when you run the command sudo smartctl -a /dev/sda, it will display information about the status of the storage device. The output may look like this:

```
smartctl 7.1 2019-12-30 r5022 [x86_64-linux-5.4.0-42-generic] (local build)
Copyright (C) 2002-19, Bruce Allen, Christian Franke, www.smartmontools.org

=== START OF INFORMATION SECTION ===
Model Family:     Seagate Barracuda 7200.14 (AF)
Device Model:     ST2000DM006-2DM164
Serial Number:    Z1E1SZ5S
LU WWN Device Id: 5 000c50 0c3a8f8e3
Firmware Version: CC43
User Capacity:    2,000,398,934,016 bytes [2.00 TB]
Sector Size:      512 bytes logical/physical
Rotation Rate:    7200 rpm
Device is:        In smartctl database [for details use: -P show]
ATA Version is:   ACS-2 (minor revision not indicated)
SATA Version is:  SATA 3.0, 6.0 Gb/s (current: 6.0 Gb/s)
Local Time is:    Mon Jan 18 08:51:50 2021 UTC
SMART support is: Available - device has SMART capability.
SMART support is: Enabled
```

This output provides detailed information about the storage device, including the model, firmware version, capacity, and SMART support status. It also includes information about the current and maximum speed of the device and a lot of other details like the number of hours the device has been powered on, number of read/write operations, error count, etc.

Using 'mdadm'

This command is used to manage and monitor software RAID arrays. It can be used to detect and repair errors in RAID arrays. For example, to check the status of a RAID array on /dev/md0, you can use the command:

```
sudo mdadm --detail /dev/md0
```

when you run the command sudo mdadm --detail /dev/md0, it will display information about the RAID array on /dev/md0. The output may look like this:

```
/dev/md0:
        Version : 1.2
  Creation Time : Mon Jan 18 08:51:50 2021
     Raid Level : raid1
     Array Size : 976759936 (931.51 GiB 1000.20 GB)
  Used Dev Size : 976759936 (931.51 GiB 1000.20 GB)
   Raid Devices : 2
  Total Devices : 2
    Persistence : Superblock is persistent

    Update Time : Mon Jan 18 08:51:50 2021
          State : clean
 Active Devices : 2
Working Devices : 2
```

```
Failed Devices : 0
 Spare Devices : 0

          Name : example:0  (local to host example)
          UUID : a1b2c3d4-e5f6-g7h8-i9j0-k1l2m3n4o5p6
        Events : 0

    Number   Major   Minor   RaidDevice State
       0       8       0        0      active sync   /dev/sda
       1       8      16        1      active sync   /dev/sdb
```

This output provides detailed information about the RAID array, including the RAID level, array size, number of devices, and the status of each device in the array.

It's important to note that these commands and tools may have additional options and parameters that can be used to customize their behavior, and that different file systems may require different commands and tools to check for errors.

It's also important to note that running these commands and tools may cause data loss or file system corruption if not used properly. It's always recommended to take backup before running these commands and tools, and to use them in a test environment before applying them to a production system.

Managing Logical Volumes

Understanding Logical Volumes

Logical volumes are a way to manage storage on a system. They allow an administrator to create and manage virtual storage devices, called logical volumes, that can be created from one or more physical storage devices, such as hard drives or partitions. Logical volumes provide several advantages over traditional partitioning:

- Flexibility: Logical volumes can be resized, moved, and mirrored without having to reboot the system or unmount the file system.

- Scalability: Logical volumes can be created across multiple physical devices, allowing for the creation of large virtual storage devices.

- Performance: Logical volumes can be striped across multiple physical devices, which can improve performance for read and write operations.

- Snapshotting: Logical volume manager (LVM) allows for the creation of snapshots, which are read-only copies of a logical volume at a specific point in time. This can be useful for backups or for creating test environments.

Some common operations that an administrator may perform around Linux logical volumes include:

Creating a Logical Volume

This can be done using the lvcreate command. For example, to create a logical volume named "lvol1" with a size of 10GB from a volume group named "vg1", the command would be:

```
sudo lvcreate -L 10G -n lvol1 vg1
```

The command sudo lvcreate -L 10G -n lvol1 vg1 creates a logical volume named "lvol1" with a size of 10GB from a volume group named "vg1". The output will look like this:

```
Logical volume "lvol1" created.
```

Resizing a Logical Volume

This can be done using the lvextend command. For example, to increase the size of the logical volume "lvol1" by 5GB, the command would be:

```
sudo lvextend -L +5G /dev/vg1/lvol1
```

The command sudo lvextend -L +5G /dev/vg1/lvol1 increases the size of the logical volume "lvol1" by 5GB. The output will look like this:

```
Size of logical volume vg1/lvol1 changed from 15.00 GiB (3840
extents) to 20.00 GiB (5120 extents).
Logical volume vg1/lvol1 successfully resized.
```

Creating a Snapshot of a Logical Volume

This can be done using the lvcreate command with the -s option. For example, to create a snapshot of the logical volume "lvol1" named "lvol1_snap", the command would be:

```
sudo lvcreate -L 10G -s -n lvol1_snap /dev/vg1/lvol1
```

The command sudo lvcreate -L 10G -s -n lvol1_snap /dev/vg1/lvol1 creates a snapshot of the logical volume "lvol1" named "lvol1_snap" with a size of 10GB. The output will look like this:

```
Logical volume "lvol1_snap" created.
```

Removing a Logical Volume

This can be done using the lvremove command. For example, to remove the logical volume "lvol1", the command would be:

```
sudo lvremove /dev/vg1/lvol1
```

The command sudo lvremove /dev/vg1/lvol1 removes the logical volume "lvol1". The output will look like this:

```
Logical volume "lvol1" successfully removed
```

Viewing Information on Logical Volumes

This can be done using the lvdisplay command. For example, to view information about all logical volumes in the volume group "vg1", the command would be:

```
sudo lvdisplay /dev/vg1
```

The command sudo lvdisplay /dev/vg1 displays information about all logical volumes in the volume group "vg1". The output will look like this:

```
  --- Logical volume ---
  LV Path                /dev/vg1/lvol1
  LV Name                lvol1
  VG Name                vg1
  LV UUID                lVjcQ1-z5nZ-K
```

It's important to note that these commands and options may have additional parameters and options that can be used to customize their behavior, and that different LVM version may require different commands and options.

It's also important to note that running these commands may cause data loss or file system corruption if not used properly. It's always recommended to take backup before running these commands and tools, and to use them in a test environment before applying them to a production system.

Hack#1: Working Around Disk Partitioning

- Always make a backup of your important data before making any changes to the partition table.

- Plan your partition layout carefully, taking into account the size and number of partitions, the filesystem type, and the intended use of each partition.

- Use a partitioning tool that supports your filesystem and your hardware, such as GPT for UEFI systems and MBR for BIOS systems.

- Use a partitioning tool that allows you to resize, move, or merge partitions without losing data, such as GParted or Parted.

- Use a partitioning tool that allows you to create and delete partitions, format them with the desired filesystem, and set their mount point.

Hack#2: Checking File System Errors

- Check the filesystem regularly for errors using the fsck (file system check) tool.

- Use a filesystem that supports journaling to reduce the risk of data loss and to speed up the recovery process.

- Use a filesystem that supports snapshots to create point-in-time backups of your data and to rollback to a previous state.

- Use a filesystem that supports encryption to protect your data from unauthorized access.

- Use a filesystem that supports compression to save disk space and to reduce the load on the disk.

Hack#3: Logical Volume Management

- Use a logical volume manager (LVM) that allows you to create, resize, and delete logical volumes, and to format them with the desired filesystem.

- Use a LVM that allows you to create and delete snapshots of your logical volumes, and to rollback to a previous state.

- Use a LVM that allows you to mirror or RAID your logical volumes, and to increase the availability and the performance of your data.

- Use a LVM that allows you to encrypt your logical volumes, and to protect your data from unauthorized access.

- Use a LVM that allows you to compress your logical volumes, and to save disk space and to reduce the load on the disk.

It is important to note that disk partitioning and logical volume management are sensitive tasks, and it is important to make sure you understand the implications of your changes before you proceed. It is also important to regularly check the filesystems for errors and to use a filesystem that supports journaling and snapshots. Furthermore, LVM allows more flexibility in managing and organizing storage, it is also important to backup data before making any changes to the LVM and regularly check the LVM for any errors. It is also important to stay updated on the latest threats and vulnerabilities, and to be familiar with the laws and regulations that may apply to your organization while working around disk partitioning, filesystem errors and logical volume management.

Chapter 8: Working around Proxy Servers

Understanding Proxy Server

A proxy server is a software solution that acts as an intermediary between clients and other service servers. Instead of reaching the servers directly, the clients must connect to the proxy server and ask it to forward their requests to the actual servers. The figure below shows the schematic of a regular Internet access proxy server, detailing how the connections compare with a non-proxied connection:

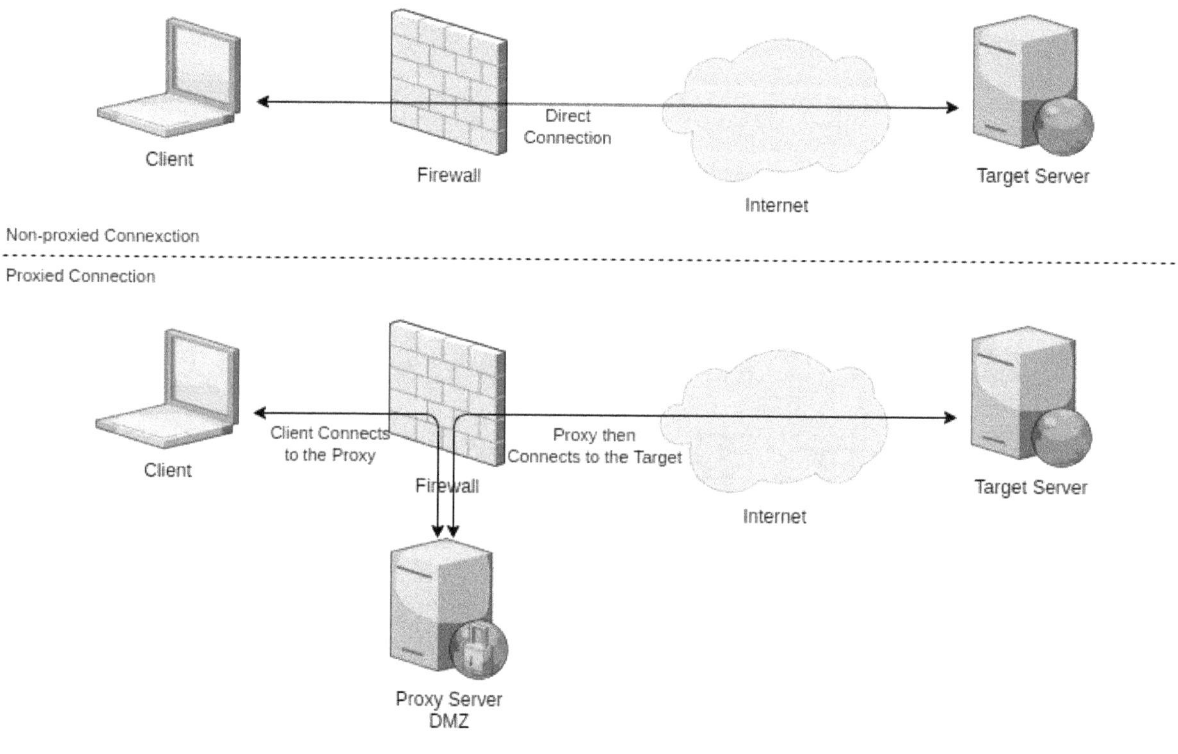

As we can see, the proxy relays messages between two connections, mimicking the actual server to the client.

Many corporate environments use proxy servers to control their Internet traffic better. Proxy servers can cache Internet resources, reduce bandwidth needs by compressing data streams, and do advanced content-based web filtering. They can even improve privacy by masking metadata within the stream. Unfortunately, it's hard to run Linux smoothly behind web proxies without messing with a lot of configuration.

Overview of Proxy Server Commands

There are several relevant proxy server-related commands that Linux administrators can use to manage and monitor proxy servers, here are some common examples:

- squid: This command is used to start, stop, and reload the Squid proxy server.
- haproxy: This command is used to start, stop, and reload the HAProxy proxy server.
- nginx: This command is used to start, stop, and reload the Nginx proxy server.
- telnet: This command can be used to test if a proxy server is reachable and if it's configured correctly.
- curl: This command can be used to test a proxy server by sending a request through the proxy.
- tcpdump: This command can be used to capture and analyze network traffic going through a proxy server.
- iptables: This command can be used to configure firewall rules for a proxy server, such as allowing or blocking specific IP addresses or ports.
- export: This command is used to set environment variables for proxy server settings, such as HTTP_PROXY, HTTPS_PROXY, and NO_PROXY.
- netstat: This command can be used to view the connections and status of a proxy server, such as which ports are listening.
- systemctl: This command is used to start, stop, restart and check the status of proxy servers running as a service, such as Squid, HAProxy, Nginx

Setting Up Proxy Server

Setting up a proxy server involves configuring a server to act as a middleman for network traffic. The server receives requests from clients, such as web browsers, and forwards them to the appropriate destination, such as a web server.

The proxy server can be used to provide various services, such as:

- Caching: By caching frequently requested content, the proxy server can reduce the load on the origin server and improve response times for clients.
- Filtering: The proxy server can be configured to block or allow specific types of traffic, based on rules and policies set by the administrator.
- Anonymity: The proxy server can be used to hide the IP addresses of clients, providing anonymity for users.
- Access control: The proxy server can be configured to require authentication for certain types of traffic, and can be used to restrict access to certain websites or services.
- Logging: The proxy server can be configured to log all requests and responses, providing valuable information for troubleshooting and monitoring.

Following is an example of how to set up a Squid proxy server on Ubuntu:

Install Squid: The first step is to install the Squid package by running the command

```
sudo apt-get install squid
```

Configure Squid: Next, we need to configure Squid by editing the configuration file located at /etc/squid/squid.conf. The file contains a lot of options and settings that you can configure, such as the port to listen on, the IP addresses that are allowed to connect, and the type of traffic to allow or block.

Start Squid: Once the configuration is done, we can start Squid by running the command

```
sudo systemctl start squid
```

Test Squid: To test the proxy server, you can use the curl command and specifying the proxy server IP address and port.

Configure client: The final step is to configure the clients to use the proxy server. This can be done by configuring the browser settings on the client machine, or by configuring a DHCP or DNS server to automatically configure clients.

Managing Proxy Server Rules and Policies

Setting up and managing proxy server rules and policies in a Linux system typically involves editing the configuration file for the proxy server software and specifying the rules and policies to be applied. The specific steps will vary depending on the type of proxy server software you're using. Following is a general guide on how to set up and manage proxy server rules and policies for a Squid proxy server:

Edit the Configuration File

The configuration file for Squid is typically located at /etc/squid/squid.conf. This file contains a lot of options and settings that you can configure, such as the port to listen on, the IP addresses that are allowed to connect, and the type of traffic to allow or block.

Following is an example of how to edit the configuration file for a Squid proxy server on a Linux system:

- Open the configuration file: The configuration file for Squid is typically located at /etc/squid/squid.conf. You can open the file using a text editor, such as nano or vi. For example, you can use the command sudo nano /etc/squid/squid.conf to open the file in the nano editor.
- Make changes: Once the file is open, you can make changes to the various options and settings. For example, you can specify the port that the proxy server should listen on by editing the line http_port 3128
- Save the changes: Once you've made your changes, you need to save the file. In nano, you can save the file by pressing Ctrl+O and then exit the editor by pressing Ctrl+X.

- Reload the proxy server: After making changes to the configuration file, you need to reload the proxy server for the new configuration to take effect. You can use the command sudo systemctl reload squid to reload the proxy server.

- Test the changes: To test the changes, you can use the curl command and specifying the proxy server IP address and port.

Setup Access Controls

One of the most important aspects of managing proxy server rules and policies is setting up access controls. You can specify which IP addresses or hostnames are allowed to connect to the proxy server, and which are not. You can also specify which types of traffic are allowed or blocked.

Following is an example of how to set up access controls for a Squid proxy server on a Linux system:

- Open the configuration file: The configuration file for Squid is typically located at /etc/squid/squid.conf. You can open the file using a text editor, such as nano or vi. For example, you can use the command sudo nano /etc/squid/squid.conf to open the file in the nano editor.

- Create an ACL: To set up access controls, you will need to create an ACL. An ACL is a list of IP addresses, hostnames, or other criteria that you want to allow or deny access to the proxy server. You can create an ACL by adding a line in the configuration file, such as acl allowed_hosts src 1.2.3.4/32 which allows the IP address 1.2.3.4 to connect to the proxy server.

- Use http_access: Once the ACL is created, you can use the http_access directive to specify which IP addresses or hostnames are allowed or denied. For example, you can use the line http_access allow allowed_hosts to allow access to the IP addresses or hostnames specified in the allowed_hosts ACL.

- Save the changes: Once you've made your changes, you need to save the file. In nano, you can save the file by pressing Ctrl+O and then exit the editor by pressing Ctrl+X.

- Reload the proxy server: After making changes to the configuration file, you need to reload the proxy server for the new configuration to take effect. You can use the command sudo systemctl reload squid to reload the proxy server.

- Test the access controls: To test the access controls, you can use the curl command and specifying the proxy server IP address and port. You can try to connect to the proxy server from an IP address or hostname that is not allowed, and confirm that the connection is denied.

Create ACL

Access control lists (ACL) are used to define rules for different types of traffic, such as HTTP or HTTPS. An ACL can be defined by creating an access list file, and then referencing that file in the configuration file.

Following is an example of how to create Access Control Lists (ACLs) for a Squid proxy server on a Linux system:

- Open the configuration file: The configuration file for Squid is typically located at /etc/squid/squid.conf. You can open the file using a text editor, such as nano or vi. For example, you can use the command sudo nano /etc/squid/squid.conf to open the file in the nano editor.

- Define the ACL: To create an ACL, you need to specify the type of criteria you want to use and give it a name. Squid supports various types of criteria such as "src" for IP addresses, "dst" for destination addresses, "url_regex" for URL patterns and "user" for username and "method" for http request methods.

For example:

```
acl allowed_hosts src 1.2.3.4/32
acl blocked_hosts src 1.2.3.5/32
acl specific_urls url_regex -i "/etc/squid/allowed_urls.txt"
acl specific_users user admin
```

- Use the ACL: Once the ACL is created, you can use it in the http_access directive to specify which IP addresses, hostnames, url patterns, users or request methods are allowed or denied. For example, you can use the line http_access allow allowed_hosts to allow access to the IP addresses specified in the allowed_hosts ACL, or http_access deny blocked_hosts to deny access to the IP addresses specified in the blocked_hosts ACL.

- Save the changes: Once you've made your changes, you need to save the file. In nano, you can save the file by pressing Ctrl+O and then exit the editor by pressing Ctrl+X.

- Reload the proxy server: After making changes to the configuration file, you need to reload the proxy server for the new configuration to take effect. You can use the command `sudo systemctl reload squid` to reload the proxy server.

- Test the ACLs: To test the ACLs, you can use the curl command and specifying the proxy server IP address and port. You can try to connect to the proxy server from an IP address or hostname that is not allowed, and confirm that the connection is denied. You can also test the url patterns, users, and request methods by sending requests to the proxy server and checking the logs to see if the requests are being allowed or denied based on the ACLs you have set up.

Use 'http_access'

http_access directive is used to define the rules for what traffic is allowed or denied. You can use the http_access allow and http_access deny directives to specify which IP addresses or hostnames are allowed or denied.

Following is an example of how to define traffic rules using the http_access directive for a Squid proxy server on a Linux system:

- Open the configuration file: The configuration file for Squid is typically located at /etc/squid/squid.conf. You can open the file using a text editor, such as nano or vi. For example, you can use the command sudo nano /etc/squid/squid.conf to open the file in the nano editor.

- Use the http_access directive: Once the configuration file is open, you can use the http_access directive to specify the rules for what traffic is allowed or denied. You can use the http_access allow and http_access deny directives to specify which IP addresses, hostnames, url patterns, users, or request methods are allowed or denied.

For example:

```
http_access allow allowed_hosts
http_access deny blocked_hosts
http_access allow specific_urls
```

```
http_access deny specific_users
http_access allow specific_methods
```

- Save the changes: Once you've made your changes, you need to save the file. In nano, you can save the file by pressing Ctrl+O and then exit the editor by pressing Ctrl+X.

- Reload the proxy server: After making changes to the configuration file, you need to reload the proxy server for the new configuration to take effect. You can use the command sudo systemctl reload squid to reload the proxy server.

- Test the traffic rules: To test the traffic rules, you can use the curl command and specifying the proxy server IP address and port. You can try to connect to the proxy server from an IP address or hostname that is not allowed, and confirm that the connection is denied. You can also test the url patterns, users, and request methods by sending requests to the proxy server and checking the logs to see if the requests are being allowed or denied based on the rules you have set up.

Setup Caching

Another important aspect of managing proxy server rules and policies is setting up caching. You can configure Squid to cache frequently requested content, which can reduce the load on the origin server and improve response times for clients.

Following is an example of how to set up caching for a Squid proxy server on a Linux system:

- Open the configuration file: The configuration file for Squid is typically located at /etc/squid/squid.conf. You can open the file using a text editor, such as nano or vi. For example, you can use the command sudo nano /etc/squid/squid.conf to open the file in the nano editor.

- Specify the cache directory: To set up caching, you need to specify the directory where the cached content will be stored. You can specify the directory by editing the line cache_dir ufs /var/spool/squid 100 16 256 in the configuration file. The directory path is /var/spool/squid, the maximum size of the cache directory is 100MB and it can contain up to 16 subdirectories with a maximum of 256 files per subdirectory.

- Set the cache size: You can set the maximum size of the cache by editing the cache_mem line in the configuration file. For example, you can set the cache size to 64MB by editing the line cache_mem 64 MB.

- Set the minimum object size: You can set the minimum size of an object that will be cached by editing the minimum_object_size line in the configuration file. For example, you can set the minimum object size to 64KB by editing the line minimum_object_size 64 KB.

- Save the changes: Once you've made your changes, you need to save the file. In nano, you can save the file by pressing Ctrl+O and then exit the editor by pressing Ctrl+X.

- Reload the proxy server: After making changes to the configuration file, you need to reload the proxy server for the new configuration to take effect. You can use the command sudo systemctl reload squid to reload the proxy server.

- Test the caching: To test the caching, you can use the curl command and specifying the proxy server IP address and port. You can also check the cache directory to see if the content is being cached, and check the logs to see if the cached content is being served to clients.

Reload the Proxy Server

After making changes to the configuration file, you need to reload the proxy server for the new rules and policies to take effect. You can use the command sudo systemctl reload squid to reload the proxy server.

Following is an example of how to reload a Squid proxy server on a Linux system:

- Verify the status of the proxy server: Verify that the proxy server is currently running by using the command sudo systemctl status squid. This command will show the status of the proxy server and confirm that it is currently running.

- Reload the proxy server: Once you have confirmed that the proxy server is running, you can use the command sudo systemctl reload squid to reload the proxy server. This command will cause the proxy server to re-read its configuration file and apply any changes you have made.

- Verify the status of the proxy server after reload: After reloading the proxy server, you can use the command sudo systemctl status squid again to verify that the proxy server is running and that the changes have been applied.

- Test the proxy server: To test the proxy server, you can use the curl command and specifying the proxy server IP address and port.

Monitoring Proxy Server Performance

Need of Monitoring Performance

Proxy servers play a critical role in network infrastructure by providing secure and efficient access to the internet. They act as intermediaries between clients and servers, and can provide a variety of benefits including:

Security: Proxy servers can provide an additional layer of security by filtering incoming and outgoing traffic, and blocking malicious or unwanted traffic.

Caching: Proxy servers can cache frequently requested content, which can significantly improve performance by reducing the number of requests sent to the origin server.

Anonymity: Proxy servers can provide anonymity by hiding the IP addresses of clients, which can be useful for protecting privacy and bypassing geo-restrictions.

Content Filtering: Proxy servers can be used to block or restrict access to specific websites or content, which can be useful for enforcing organizational policies or protecting users from malicious content.

Load Balancing: Proxy servers can be used to distribute incoming traffic among multiple servers, which can help to improve performance and availability.

Due to the critical role that proxy servers play, it is important that they are configured and maintained properly to ensure optimal performance. This includes ensuring that the proxy server is configured to handle the expected number of users, and that the proxy server's cache is properly configured to store frequently requested content. Additionally, it is important to monitor the proxy server's performance and troubleshoot any issues that may arise.

Steps to Check Performance

Following is an example of how to monitor the performance of a Squid proxy server on a Linux system:

- Use the squidclient command: The squidclient command can be used to retrieve statistics from the proxy server. For example, you can use the command squidclient mgr:info to retrieve information about the proxy server's performance, including the number of requests, the amount of data transferred, and the number of cache hits and misses.

- Use the squidaccess.log: The squidaccess.log file contains information about the requests that the proxy server handles, including the client IP address, the request method, the requested URL, and the status of the request. You can use the command tail -f /var/log/squid/access.log to view the access log in real time.

- Use the squidcache.log: The squidcache.log file contains information about the proxy server's caching activity, including the objects that are cached and the objects that are removed from the cache. You can use the command tail -f /var/log/squid/cache.log to view the cache log in real time.

- Use the squiderror.log: The squiderror.log file contains information about errors that occur when the proxy server handles requests. You can use the command tail -f /var/log/squid/error.log to view the error log in real time.

- Use a monitoring tool: You can use a monitoring tool such as Nagios, Munin or Prometheus to monitor the performance of the proxy server. These tools provide an easy way to graph performance data and set up alerts.

- Analyze the data: Once you have collected the data, you can analyze it to identify any performance bottlenecks, such as high latency, low cache hit rate, or high error rate. You can use this information to make adjustments to the proxy server's configuration, or to identify any issues that may need to be addressed.

Managing Proxy Server Logs

Proxy server logs are records of the activity that takes place on a proxy server, such as client requests and responses, caching activity, and errors. These logs can be used to troubleshoot issues, monitor performance, and analyze traffic patterns.

Following is an example of how to pull and manage proxy server logs for a Squid proxy server on a Linux system:

- Locate the log files: In Squid, the log files are typically located in the /var/log/squid directory. The main log files are access.log, cache.log, and store.log. The access.log file contains information about client requests, the cache.log file contains information about caching activity, and the store.log file contains information about storage activity.

- Pull the logs: You can use the tail command to view the logs in real-time, for example tail -f /var/log/squid/access.log will show the access log in real-time. Or you can use the cat command to view the entire log file, for example cat /var/log/squid/access.log will show the entire access log.

- Rotate the logs: To prevent log files from growing too large and consuming too much disk space, you can use log rotation tools such as logrotate to rotate and compress the logs. This will keep the log files at a manageable size and make it easier to analyze the data.

- Analyze the logs: Once you have collected the logs, you can analyze them to identify any performance bottlenecks, such as high latency, low cache hit rate, or high error rate. You can use tools like grep, awk or sed to filter and extract relevant information from the logs.

- Use a log analyzer: You can use a log analyzer tool such as Squid log analyzer or GoAccess to make sense of the log data, providing a more visual representation of the data. These tools can help you to identify patterns in the data and generate useful statistics.

- Monitor the logs: You can use a log monitoring tool such as Logstash, Fluentd, or Elasticsearch to monitor the logs in real-time. These tools can automatically detect and alert on unusual patterns or anomalies in the logs, which can help you to identify and troubleshoot issues more quickly.

- Store the logs: To keep a historical record of the logs, it is best to store them in a centralized log management system, like a log aggregator, for long-term storage and analysis. This allows you to keep track of historical data and perform forensic analysis when needed.

- Make use of the logs: The logs can be used for different purposes like:
  - Auditing: The logs can be used to track user activity and identify any suspicious or malicious behavior.
  - Troubleshooting: The logs can be used to diagnose and troubleshoot issues with the proxy server or the network.
  - Performance monitoring: The logs can be used to monitor the performance of the proxy server and identify any bottlenecks or issues that may need to be addressed.
  - Compliance: The logs can be used to comply with regulatory requirements or organizational policies.

Updating Proxy Server

Need of Update to Proxy Server

Updating a proxy server is important for several reasons:

- Security: Updates often include security patches that address known vulnerabilities and fix security issues. By keeping your proxy server updated, you can help to protect your network from potential security breaches.

- Performance: Updates may include performance improvements and new features that can help to improve the performance of your proxy server.

- Compatibility: Updates may include changes that improve compatibility with other software or devices.

Steps to Update Proxy Server

Following is an example of how to update a Squid proxy server on a Linux system:

- Check the version of Squid: To check the current version of Squid, you can use the command squid -v. This will display the version of Squid currently installed on your system.

- Download the latest version: You can download the latest version of Squid from the official website http://www.squid-cache.org/ or through the package manager of your Linux distribution.

- Stop the Squid service: Before updating, the Squid service should be stopped. You can use the command sudo systemctl stop squid to stop the service.

- Install the update: Once the package has been downloaded, you can use the package manager of your Linux distribution to install the update. For example, on Debian-based systems, you can use the command sudo apt-get install squid to install the update.

- Configure the new version: After the update, you should review the new configuration options and make any necessary changes to the configuration file.

- Start the Squid service: Finally, the Squid service should be started again using the command sudo systemctl start squid

- Verify the version of Squid: Verify that the update was successful by running the command squid -v again, which should display the new version of Squid.

Configuring Proxy Server Clients

A proxy server client is a device or software that connects to a proxy server in order to access the internet or other network resources. Clients can include computers, smartphones, tablets, and other devices that are configured to use a proxy server.

Steps to Create, Configure and Manage Proxy Clients

Following is an example of how to create, configure, and administer proxy server clients for a Squid proxy server on a Linux system:

Configure the client: On the client device, configure the proxy server settings by specifying the IP address and port number of the proxy server. The client should be configured to use the proxy server for all internet traffic.

Create an ACL: On the proxy server, create an access control list (ACL) to specify which clients are allowed to connect to the proxy server. This can be done by editing the Squid configuration file and adding the IP addresses or subnets of the clients that are allowed to connect.

Configure authentication: If you want to require authentication for the clients, you can configure the proxy server to use an authentication method such as basic authentication or NTLM. This can be done by editing the Squid configuration file and specifying the authentication method and any necessary credentials.

Create a cache rule: On the proxy server, create a cache rule to specify how the proxy server should handle caching for the clients. This can be done by editing the Squid configuration file and adding a cache rule that specifies the clients or subnets that the rule applies to, and the caching behavior for those clients.

Monitor the clients: Monitor the clients to ensure that they are connecting to the proxy server correctly and that their traffic is being handled as expected. This can be done by viewing the logs on the proxy server, or by using a monitoring tool.

Administer the clients: You can administer the clients by setting up policies, like which websites they can access, which they can't, or how much traffic they can use, etc.

Hack#1: Using Proxy Servers:

- Use a reputable proxy service that has a clear and comprehensive privacy policy.
- Use a proxy service that supports the protocols you need to use, such as HTTP, HTTPS, and SOCKS.
- Use a proxy service that offers a large number of servers to reduce the chances of over-crowding and slow connection speeds.

- Use a proxy service that offers a kill switch feature to protect your IP in case the proxy connection drops.
- Use a proxy service that offers a no-logs policy to protect your data from being tracked.

Hack#2: Best Practices on Proxy Server Logs:

- Use a proxy service that offers detailed logging options to help you monitor and troubleshoot network issues.
- Use a log analysis tool to process the logs and extract useful information, such as the most active users, the most accessed resources, and the most common errors.
- Use a log visualization tool to create charts and graphs that can help you identify patterns and trends in the log data.
- Use a log archiving tool to store the logs for a longer period of time, in case you need to refer back to them later.
- Use a log security tool to encrypt the logs and protect them from unauthorized access.

Hack#3: Performance of Proxy Servers:

- Use a proxy service that offers servers in locations close to your physical location to reduce latency and increase connection speed.
- Use a proxy service that offers unlimited bandwidth to avoid throttling or disconnections.
- Use a proxy service that offers a caching feature to reduce the load on the origin server and improve the performance.
- Use a proxy service that offers load balancing to distribute the traffic among multiple servers and improve the performance.

- Use a proxy service that offers a monitoring feature to check the availability and the performance of the servers and the proxy service.

It is important to note that proxy servers can be a useful tool for privacy and security, but it is important to use a reputable service and to regularly monitor the proxy connection, its configuration and its performance. It is also important to be aware of the laws and regulations that may apply to your organization while using proxy servers. Additionally, it is important to use a secure way to handle the logs, to keep them for a long enough period and to use the logs to improve the security and the performance of the proxy service.

CHAPTER 9: ADMINISTERING VPNs

Overview of Popular VPN Protocols

VPN protocols are the methods used to establish and maintain a secure connection between a VPN client and server. There are several different VPN protocols available, each with its own set of features and benefits. Following is an overview of some of the most common VPN protocols:

1. PPTP (Point-to-Point Tunneling Protocol): PPTP is one of the oldest and most widely supported VPN protocols. It is supported by most operating systems and devices, and is relatively easy to set up. However, PPTP is not considered very secure and is vulnerable to various types of attacks.

2. L2TP (Layer 2 Tunneling Protocol): L2TP is a more secure version of PPTP, and is often used in combination with Internet Protocol Security (IPSec) to provide encryption and authentication. L2TP is also widely supported, but can be more difficult to set up than PPTP.

3. SSTP (Secure Socket Tunneling Protocol): SSTP is a Microsoft-developed VPN protocol that is similar to PPTP and L2TP. It is considered more secure than PPTP and is supported by Windows operating systems.

4. OpenVPN: OpenVPN is an open-source VPN protocol that is considered to be one of the most secure and versatile VPN protocols available. It is supported by most operating systems, and can be configured to use a variety of encryption and authentication methods.

5. IKEv2 (Internet Key Exchange version 2): IKEv2 is a newer VPN protocol that is considered to be very fast and secure. It is supported by most operating systems and is particularly well-suited for mobile devices.

6. WireGuard: WireGuard is a relatively new and lightweight VPN protocol, that is considered to be very fast and secure. It is supported by multiple operating systems, and is particularly well-suited for mobile devices.

Each VPN protocol has its own advantages and disadvantages. In general, OpenVPN and IKEv2 are considered to be the most secure and versatile protocols, while PPTP is considered to be the least secure. WireGuard is considered to be lightweight and fast VPN protocol. The best choice of protocol will depend on the specific requirements of your organization.

Selection Factors for VPN

When selecting a VPN protocol, there are several factors to consider:

- Security: The level of security provided by a VPN protocol is an important factor to consider. OpenVPN and IKEv2 are considered to be the most secure protocols, while PPTP is considered to be the least secure.

- Compatibility: It is important to ensure that the VPN protocol you choose is compatible with the devices and operating systems that you will be using. Some protocols, such as PPTP and L2TP, are widely supported, while others, such as SSTP, are only supported by certain operating systems.

- Performance: The performance of a VPN protocol can be affected by factors such as encryption and authentication methods, as well as the number of users connected to the VPN. WireGuard is considered to be a lightweight and fast VPN protocol.

- Use case: Different protocols may be better suited for different use cases. For example, IKEv2 is particularly well-suited for mobile devices, while OpenVPN is more versatile and can be used in a variety of scenarios.

- Support: It is important to consider the level of support and documentation available for the VPN protocol you choose. OpenVPN is an open-source protocol, which means that tFollowing is a large community of developers and users who can provide support and documentation.

- Other specific requirements: Some protocols may provide features that are important for your organization, such as the ability to bypass firewalls or geo-restrictions.

Ultimately, the best choice of VPN protocol will depend on the specific requirements of your organization. It is recommended to test different protocols and compare their performance and security features before making a decision.

Installing VPN

Use of VPNs

VPN (Virtual Private Network) is a technology that allows users to create a secure connection to another network over the internet. A VPN creates a virtual "tunnel" through which data can be transmitted securely and privately. This allows users to access resources on a remote network as if they were directly connected to it, such as accessing a company's internal network while working remotely.

VPNs are used for a variety of purposes, including:

- providing secure remote access to a company's internal network for remote workers or mobile users
- Encrypting internet traffic to protect it from snooping or tampering
- Bypassing internet censorship or geo-restrictions to access blocked websites or services
- Hiding a user's true IP address and location to enhance privacy and security

Types of VPNs

There are two types of VPNs, including:

1. Remote Access VPNs: These VPNs allow users to connect to a remote network from anywhere. These types of VPNs are often used by remote workers and mobile users.
2. Site-to-Site VPNs: These VPNs connect multiple networks together, allowing users on one network to access resources on another network. These types of VPNs are often used by businesses to connect branch offices together.

Installing OpenVPN on Ubuntu

Following is a step-by-step guide on how to install OpenVPN on Ubuntu 20.04:

Install the OpenVPN package: Open the terminal and run the command sudo apt-get install openvpn. This will install the OpenVPN package and all the necessary dependencies.

Generate the CA and server and client certificates: Create a directory for storing the certificate files, such as /etc/openvpn/easy-rsa/. Inside the directory, copy the easy-rsa script using cp -r /usr/share/easy-rsa/ /etc/openvpn/.

Create the server and client certificates:

Change the directory to /etc/openvpn/easy-rsa/ using cd /etc/openvpn/easy-rsa/.

Run the command source vars to set the environment variables for the certificate generation.

Run the command ./clean-all to clean any previous certificates.

Run the command ./build-ca to generate the root CA.

Run the command ./build-key-server server to generate the server certificate.

Run the command ./build-dh to generate the Diffie-Hellman parameters.

Run the command ./build-key client1 to generate the client certificate.

Create the server configuration file: Create a server configuration file in /etc/openvpn/ using sudo nano /etc/openvpn/server.conf

Add the following lines:

```
port 1194
proto udp
dev tun
ca /etc/openvpn/easy-rsa/keys/ca.crt
cert /etc/openvpn/easy-rsa/keys/server.crt
key /etc/openvpn/easy-rsa/keys/server.key
dh /etc/openvpn/easy-rsa/keys/dh2048.pem
server 10.8.0.0 255.255.255.0
```

```
ifconfig-pool-pers
ist ipp.txt
push "redirect-gateway def1 bypass-dhcp"
push "dhcp-option DNS 8.8.8.8"
push "dhcp-option DNS 8.8.4.4"
keepalive 10 120
cipher AES-256-CBC
comp-lzo
user nobody
group nogroup
persist-key
persist-tun
status openvpn-status.log
verb 3
```

- The above configuration is for a basic OpenVPN server using the UDP protocol on port 1194, with the TUN device and AES-256-CBC encryption. Please note that this is a basic example, and you may want to customize the settings according to your needs.

Configure the firewall:
- Allow incoming traffic on port 1194 using `sudo ufw allow 1194/udp`
- Enable the firewall using `sudo ufw enable`

Start the OpenVPN service:
- Start the OpenVPN service using `sudo systemctl start openvpn@server`
- Enable the OpenVPN service to start automatically on boot using `sudo systemctl enable openvpn@server`

Test the OpenVPN connection:

- On the client machine, install the OpenVPN client using `sudo apt-get install openvpn`
- Copy the client certificate and key files to the client machine
- Create a client configuration file, usually /etc/openvpn/client.conf, and configure the settings such as the server's IP address and port number, the location of the certificate and key files, and the encryption settings.
- Connect to the OpenVPN server using the command `sudo openvpn --config /etc/openvpn/client.conf`

You should now be connected to the OpenVPN server. You can check the connection status by running the command `sudo systemctl status openvpn@server`.

Securing VPN Connections

Threat to VPNs

VPN (Virtual Private Network) connections are used to establish a secure and private connection between a user and a remote network. By encrypting and tunneling internet traffic through a VPN, users can protect their data from snooping and tampering, and access resources on remote networks as if they were directly connected to it.

One of the main reasons to secure VPN connections is to protect sensitive information from being intercepted and compromised by hackers or other malicious actors. VPNs encrypt internet traffic, making it unreadable to anyone who intercepts it. This is especially important when using public Wi-Fi networks, which are often unsecured and vulnerable to attacks.

Another benefit of VPN connections is that they can help to hide a user's true IP address and location, making it more difficult for hackers or other malicious actors to track or target them. This can be especially useful for users who want to access blocked websites or services, or for those who want to protect their privacy online.

VPNs also provide a way for remote workers and mobile users to securely access a company's internal network and resources. This can be especially useful for companies with employees who travel frequently or work remotely. By providing remote workers with a VPN connection, companies can ensure that their data and resources are protected, even when accessed from outside the office.

In addition, VPNs can also help to improve network performance by reducing the amount of traffic that needs to be sent over the public internet. This can be especially useful for companies with branch offices or other remote locations that need to connect to a central network.

Furthermore, VPNs can also help to protect against Distributed Denial of Service (DDoS) attacks by routing traffic through multiple VPN servers. DDoS attacks are a common form of cyber attack in which hackers flood a network or website with fake traffic, causing it to become overwhelmed and unavailable. By routing traffic through multiple VPN servers, it becomes more difficult for hackers to target a specific server or network.

Overall, VPN connections provide a way for users to securely and privately access the internet and remote networks. They can protect sensitive information from being intercepted and compromised, hide a user's true IP address and location, and provide a secure way for remote workers and mobile users to access a company's internal network and resources. Additionally, VPNs can also improve network performance and protect against DDoS attacks.

Steps to Secure VPN Connections

Following is a step-by-step guide on how to secure an OpenVPN connection:

- Enable encryption: OpenVPN supports a variety of encryption algorithms, including AES-256-CBC, AES-128-CBC, and BF-CBC. To enable encryption, you will need to add the appropriate encryption algorithm to the server configuration file, usually located at /etc/openvpn/server.conf. For example, to enable AES-256-CBC encryption, you would add the line cipher AES-256-CBC to the server configuration file.

- Enable authentication: OpenVPN supports several authentication methods, including pre-shared keys, certificates, and username/password authentication. To enable authentication, you will need to add the appropriate authentication method to the server configuration file. For example, to enable certificate-based authentication, you would add the lines ca /etc/openvpn/ca.crt, cert /etc/openvpn/server.crt, and key /etc/openvpn/server.key to the server configuration file.

- Enable a firewall: A firewall can help to protect your server from unauthorized access. You can use a firewall software such as ufw, which is default firewall for Ubuntu. To enable ufw, you can use the command sudo ufw enable

- Enable port forwarding: Port forwarding can help to ensure that incoming VPN traffic is directed to the correct server. You can enable port forwarding on your router or firewall.

- Enable a VPN kill switch: A VPN kill switch is a feature that will automatically disconnect your device from the internet if the VPN connection is lost. This can help to prevent your device from accidentally connecting to an unsecured network.

- Enable a DNS leak protection: DNS leak protection can help to prevent your device from accidentally sending DNS requests outside of the VPN tunnel. This can help to protect your privacy and prevent your location from being revealed.

- Keep your OpenVPN server software up to date: OpenVPN releases updates that fix vulnerabilities and add new features. It's important to keep the OpenVPN server software up to date in order to protect against new security threats and to ensure that the software is running optimally.

- Keep your server and clients updated with the latest security patches: Keeping your server and clients updated with the latest security patches is an important aspect of securing your VPN connection. This can help to protect against vulnerabilities and other security threats.

- Regularly monitor the VPN server logs: Regularly monitoring the VPN server logs can help to detect any suspicious activity or unauthorized access attempts.

Managing VPN User Accounts

Managing VPN user accounts is an important aspect of securing and maintaining a VPN server. Following is a step-by-step guide on how to manage VPN user accounts in detail:

- Create user accounts: The first step in managing VPN user accounts is to create them. This can be done using the command line or through a web-based interface. For example, to create a user account using the command line, you can use the command sudo adduser <username>

- Assign user permissions: After creating user accounts, you will need to assign appropriate permissions to each user. This can be done by creating different groups and assigning users to them. For example, you can create a group for administrators, a group for regular users, and a group for guests.

- Create and distribute client certificates: To authenticate VPN clients, you will need to create and distribute client certificates. This can be done using the openvpn-pki tool. For example, to create a client certificate, you can use the command:

```
sudo openvpn-pki --gen-req --days 3650 <clientname>
```

- Configure client settings: After creating and distributing client certificates, you will need to configure client settings. This can be done by creating a client configuration file, usually located at /etc/openvpn/client.conf.

- Monitor user activity: It is important to monitor user activity to ensure that VPN users are not violating any policies or security rules. This can be done by regularly checking the VPN server logs or by using a monitoring tool.

- Revoke user access: If a user's access is no longer needed or if a user is found to be violating policies or security rules, their access can be revoked. This can be done by disabling their user account or by revoking their client certificate.

- Rotate certificates: To ensure the security of the VPN server, it is important to rotate certificates regularly. This can be done by creating new client certificates and distributing them to VPN clients.

- Backup and restore user accounts: It is important to create a backup of the VPN user accounts and configurations. This can be done by exporting the user accounts and configurations to a file. In the event of a server failure or other disaster, this file can be used to restore the user accounts and configurations.

- Use a VPN Authentication Server: To simplify the management of VPN user accounts, you can use a VPN Authentication Server. This is a separate server that is responsible for managing the user accounts and authentication. This can include tasks such as creating and managing user accounts, issuing and revoking client certificates, and monitoring user activity. This approach can be beneficial as it can help to centralize the management of VPN user accounts, and make it easier to scale and secure the VPN server.

- Implement two-factor authentication: To further secure VPN user accounts, you can implement two-factor authentication. This adds an additional layer of security by requiring users to provide a second form of authentication, such as a one-time code sent to their phone, in addition to their username and password. This can help to prevent unauthorized access to VPN user accounts and can be implemented using a software such as Google Authenticator.

It is important to note that the specific steps and configuration for managing VPN user accounts will depend on the VPN server software and the Linux distribution that you are using. It is always best to refer to the official documentation for your VPN server software for detailed instructions and to check for any security and compatibility issues. Additionally, it is important to establish and enforce strict policies and guidelines for managing VPN user accounts, including password policies, access controls, and logging requirements.

explain monitoring server performance in detail in 1000 words. Also show me practically how to monitor it

Monitoring Server Performance

Steps to Monitor Server Performance

Monitoring server performance is an important aspect of maintaining and optimizing the performance of a server. It can help to detect and troubleshoot issues, identify bottlenecks, and plan for future upgrades.

Following is a detailed explanation of monitoring server performance and a guide on how to do it:

- Resource utilization: The first step in monitoring server performance is to monitor the utilization of resources such as CPU, memory, storage, and network. This can be done using command line tools such as top, htop, and sar. For example, to check the current CPU utilization, you can use the command top in terminal and see the CPU usage.

- System load: The system load is a measure of how busy the system is. It can be used to identify if the system is overloaded and if so, which resources are causing the overload. This can be done using the command uptime or w which will give you the current system load.

- Network traffic: Another important aspect of monitoring server performance is to monitor the network traffic. This can help to identify bottlenecks, and plan for future upgrades. This can be done using command line tools such as netstat and iptraf.

- Disk usage: Disk usage can also be an important aspect of monitoring server performance. This can be done using command line tools such as df and du. For example, to check the current disk usage, you can use the command df -h which will give you the total disk usage in human readable format.

- Memory usage: Memory usage can also be an important aspect of monitoring server performance. This can be done using command line tools such as free, vmstat and top. For example, to check the current memory usage, you can use the command free -m which will give you the memory usage in megabytes.

- System Logs: System logs can also be an important aspect of monitoring server performance. This can be done by checking the system logs for any error messages, warning messages, and other information. This can be done using command line tools such as tail, grep, and cat.

- Automated monitoring: Automated monitoring can also be an important aspect of monitoring server performance. This can be done using monitoring tools such as Nagios, Zabbix, and Prometheus. These tools can be configured to automatically monitor server performance and send alerts when certain thresholds are exceeded.

- Performance metrics: There are several performance metrics that can be used to monitor server performance, such as CPU utilization, memory usage, disk I/O, network traffic, and system load. These metrics can be used to identify bottlenecks, plan for future upgrades, and troubleshoot issues.

- Baseline: It is important to establish a baseline of performance metrics for your server. This can be done by monitoring the server for a period of time and determining the normal ranges for the various performance metrics. This can be helpful in identifying when a performance issue occurs, as it will be easy to see when a metric deviates from the normal range.

- Track historical performance: It is also important to track historical performance over time to identify trends and patterns. This can help to identify potential issues early on and to plan for future upgrades. This can be done by storing the performance metrics in a database and using a visualization tool such as Grafana to display the data.

- Monitor specific services: In addition to monitoring the overall performance of the server, it's also important to monitor the performance of specific services that are running on the server. This can be done by monitoring the logs of the services and by using tools such as service monitoring tools like Monit, systemd, upstart.

- Identify and diagnose issues: Once an issue has been identified, it's important to diagnose the problem and determine the root cause. This can be done by using the performance metrics, system logs, and other data that have been collected.

- Plan for future upgrades: Monitoring server performance can also help to plan for future upgrades. For example, if the CPU usage is consistently high, it may be necessary to upgrade to a more powerful CPU.

To conclude, monitoring server performance is an important aspect of maintaining and optimizing the performance of a server. It can help to detect and troubleshoot issues, identify bottlenecks, and plan for future upgrades. There are a variety of tools and techniques that can be used to monitor server performance, including command line tools, monitoring tools, and performance metrics. It is important to establish a baseline of performance metrics, track historical performance, and diagnose issues when they occur. Additionally, it is essential to keep your monitoring tools and software up to date with the latest security patches.

Practical Example to Run Performance Monitoring

In practical terms, here are some examples of how to monitor server performance using some popular command line tools on a Linux system:

To monitor CPU usage:

```
top
```

To monitor memory usage:

```
free -m
```

To monitor disk usage:

```
df -h
```

To monitor network usage:

```
netstat -i
```

To monitor system load:

```
uptime
```

To monitor specific services:

```
systemctl status <service>
```

To monitor and analyze system logs:

```
tail -f /var/log/syslog
```

These are just a few examples of how to monitor server performance using command line tools. There are many other tools and techniques that can be used, such as monitoring tools like Nagios, Zabbix, and Prometheus, and performance metrics such as CPU utilization, memory usage, disk I/O, network traffic, and system load.

Tuning VPN Servers

Tuning VPN servers is an important aspect of maintaining the performance and security of a VPN server. It involves adjusting various settings and configurations to optimize the performance of the server and to ensure that it can handle the expected load.

Following is a brief explanation of VPN server tuning and some commands and tools that can be used to do it.

- Adjusting the encryption settings: To optimize the performance of a VPN server, it is important to adjust the encryption settings. This can be done by using stronger encryption algorithms or by disabling unnecessary encryption. This can be done by modifying the OpenVPN server configuration file and restarting the OpenVPN service.

- Configuring server load balancing: To ensure that the VPN server can handle the expected load, it is important to configure load balancing. This can be done by using software such as HAProxy or by using hardware load balancers. This can ensure that the VPN server is able to handle a large number of clients without overloading the system.

- Adjusting the packet size: The packet size can also affect the performance of a VPN server. This can be done by adjusting the MTU value. This can be done by modifying the OpenVPN server configuration file and restarting the OpenVPN service.

- Adjusting the number of clients: To ensure that the VPN server can handle the expected load, it is important to adjust the number of clients that can connect to the server. This can be done by modifying the OpenVPN server configuration file and restarting the OpenVPN service.

- Configuring firewall rules: To improve the security of the VPN server, it is important to configure firewall rules. This can be done by using software such as iptables. This can ensure that the VPN server is only accessible by authorized clients.

- Regularly monitoring server performance: To ensure the VPN server is running optimally, it is important to monitor the server performance regularly. This can be done by using command-line tools such as top, htop, and sar to monitor resource utilization, and by monitoring system logs to identify any issues.

- Regularly updating the VPN server: To keep the VPN server secure, it is important to regularly update the server. This can be done by using software such as yum or apt-get to update the server and by applying security patches.

- Using a VPN Authentication Server: To simplify the management of VPN user accounts, you can use a VPN Authentication Server. This is a separate server that is responsible for managing the user accounts and authentication.

In practical terms, you can use the command top to monitor server performance in real time. This command will show the current CPU, memory and swap usage, the load average and the processes that are currently running. You can press 'q' to quit the top command. The command sar is another tool that can be used to monitor server performance over a period of time, it can be run with different options to monitor various aspects of the server such as CPU, memory, network, and disk usage.

In conclusion, VPN server tuning is an important aspect of maintaining the performance and security of a VPN server. It involves adjusting various settings and configurations to optimize the performance of the server and to ensure that it can handle the expected load. Regular monitoring of server performance and updating the VPN server are also essential steps to keep the VPN server running smoothly.

Hack#1: Best Practices on VPNs:

1. Use a reputable VPN service that has a clear and comprehensive privacy policy.
2. Use a VPN protocol that is secure and well-established, such as OpenVPN or IKEv2.
3. Use a VPN service that offers a kill switch feature to protect your IP in case the VPN connection drops.
4. Use a VPN service that offers a no-logs policy to protect your data from being tracked.
5. Use a VPN service that offers DNS leak protection to prevent your DNS requests from being exposed.

Hack#2: Key Things to Secure VPNs:

1. Use a strong and unique password for your VPN account.
2. Use two-factor authentication to add an extra layer of security to your VPN login.
3. Keep your VPN software up to date to ensure that any known vulnerabilities are patched.
4. Use a firewall to protect your network while connected to a VPN.
5. Use a VPN service that offers a built-in malware and ad-blocker to protect your device from malicious content.

Hack#3: Outperforming VPNs:

1. Use a VPN service that offers servers in locations close to your physical location to reduce latency and increase connection speed.

2. Use a VPN service that offers a large number of servers to reduce the chances of over-crowding and slow connection speeds.

3. Use a VPN service that offers unlimited bandwidth to avoid throttling or disconnections.

4. Use a VPN service that offers split-tunneling to balance the VPN connection with the local connection and improve the performance.

5. Use a VPN service that offers a kill switch feature to prevent your device from leaking data in case of a VPN connection drop.

It is important to note that even with the best practices and expert tips, VPNs are not foolproof and there may still be ways for an attacker to access your data. It is important to use a reputable VPN service and to regularly monitor the VPN connection, its configuration and its performance. It is also important to stay updated on the latest threats and vulnerabilities, and to be familiar with the laws and regulations that may apply to your organization while using VPN.

Chapter 10: Working on Wireless Networks

Setting Up Wireless Access Points (WAP)

Understanding WAP

Wireless Access Points (WAPs) are devices that allow wireless devices such as smartphones, laptops, and tablets to connect to a wired network. They are an important component of a wireless network infrastructure and are necessary for creating wireless networks. In the context of Linux, WAPs can be used to create wireless networks using Linux-based operating systems, such as Ubuntu or Debian.

One of the main uses of wireless access points in networking is to provide wireless connectivity to users. This allows users to connect to a wired network without the need for physical cables, providing greater flexibility and mobility. This can be particularly useful in large buildings or outdoor areas, where running cables may be difficult or impossible.

Another use of wireless access points is to extend the reach of a wired network. Installing new network cabling can be expensive, especially in large buildings or outdoor areas. Wireless access points can be used to extend the reach of a wired network without the need for additional cabling, making it a cost-effective solution.

Wireless access points also provide security features that can protect the wireless network. They can be configured to use encryption to protect wireless communications from unauthorized access and firewalls to protect the wireless network from external attacks.

In Linux, wireless access points can be set up and configured using command-line tools such as iwconfig and iwlist. These tools can be used to configure the wireless network's SSID, password, and security settings. Additionally, Linux-based network management software, such as Network Manager or WICD, can be used to manage wireless networks and access points, making the process of setting up and managing wireless networks more user-friendly.

In conclusion, wireless access points are a key component of wireless networking, and provide the wireless connectivity that allows wireless devices to access the network and the internet. They are necessary for creating wireless networks in Linux-based operating systems and can be set up and configured using command-line tools and Linux-based network management software. They are a cost-effective solution for extending the reach of a wired network and provide security features to protect the wireless network.

Establishing Wireless Access Points

Following is a practical example of setting up a wireless access point (WAP) on a Linux-based operating system, such as Ubuntu or Debian:

First, connect the WAP to your wired network using an Ethernet cable. Make sure to connect the WAP to a switch or router that has internet connectivity.

Next, log in to the WAP's web-based management interface by entering its IP address in a web browser. The default login credentials will be provided in the WAP's manual or on the manufacturer's website.

Once logged in, navigate to the wireless settings page and configure the wireless network's SSID, which is the name that will be broadcasted for users to see and connect. Also, configure the wireless network's security settings, such as WPA or WPA2 encryption, and set a strong password for the network.

Next, navigate to the network settings page and configure the WAP's IP address, which will be used to access the management interface. It's recommended to set it as a static IP address.

Next, navigate to the firewall settings page and configure the firewall to block all incoming traffic except for the necessary ports, such as port 80 for HTTP and port 443 for HTTPS, to improve security.

Save the changes and reboot the WAP for the changes to take effect.

Once the WAP is back online, test the wireless connectivity by connecting to the wireless network using a wireless device, such as a smartphone or laptop. Verify that the wireless device can access the internet and that the wireless network's security settings are working properly.

You can also use command-line tools such as iwconfig and iwlist to check and configure the wireless network settings on the Linux machine that is connected to the WAP.

To monitor and manage the wireless network, you can use Linux-based network management software, such as Network Manager or WICD.

Repeat the process for additional WAPs if you have multiple wireless access points.

Assigning Access Points (APs)

Need of Access Points

Assigning access points means allocating specific wireless access points (WAPs) to specific areas or users within a wireless network. This is typically done in large networks with multiple WAPs, where it is important to manage and optimize wireless coverage, security, and traffic.

For example, in a large building, an administrator may assign a specific WAP to cover each floor, ensuring that all areas of the building have good wireless coverage. In a corporate environment, an administrator may assign WAPs to different departments, such as sales, marketing, and finance, to ensure that only authorized users can access the wireless network.

Assigning access points also allows an administrator to manage and optimize wireless network performance. For example, by monitoring network usage and traffic, an administrator can adjust the number of WAPs and their location to ensure that all areas of the network are receiving adequate coverage.

It also allows for better security, as an administrator can assign different levels of access to different WAPs, ensuring that only authorized users can access sensitive data and resources.

Steps to Setup and Assign Access Points

Following is a practical example of setting up and assigning access points (APs) on a Linux-based operating system, such as Ubuntu or Debian:

- First, connect the APs to your wired network using Ethernet cables. Make sure to connect them to a switch or router that has internet connectivity.
- Next, log in to the management interface of each AP by entering its IP address in a web browser. The default login credentials will be provided in the AP's manual or on the manufacturer's website.
- Once logged in, navigate to the wireless settings page and configure the wireless network's SSID, which is the name that will be broadcasted for users to see and connect. Also, configure the wireless network's security settings, such as WPA or WPA2 encryption, and set a strong password for the network.

- Next, navigate to the network settings page and configure the AP's IP address, which will be used to access the management interface. It's recommended to set it as a static IP address.

- Next, navigate to the firewall settings page and configure the firewall to block all incoming traffic except for the necessary ports, such as port 80 for HTTP and port 443 for HTTPS, to improve security.

- Save the changes and reboot the AP for the changes to take effect.

- Once the AP is back online, test the wireless connectivity by connecting to the wireless network using a wireless device, such as a smartphone or laptop. Verify that the wireless device can access the internet and that the wireless network's security settings are working properly.

- You can also use command-line tools such as iwconfig and iwlist to check and configure the wireless network settings on the Linux machine that is connected to the AP.

- To monitor and manage the wireless network, you can use Linux-based network management software, such as Network Manager or WICD.

- Repeat the process for additional APs if you have multiple access points.

- Now that all APs are up and running, you can assign them to specific areas or users within the network. For example, you can assign an AP to cover each floor of a building, or assign an AP to a specific department in a corporate environment.

- To assign an AP to a specific area or user, you can use the VLAN feature of your router or switch. You can create a VLAN for each area or user and assign the AP to the appropriate VLAN.

- You can also use a wireless controller or management software to assign APs to specific areas or users.

Steps to Manage Access Points via Terminal

Following is an example of how to set up and assign access points (APs) via the terminal on a Linux-based operating system, such as Ubuntu or Debian:

- First, connect the APs to your wired network using Ethernet cables. Make sure to connect them to a switch or router that has internet connectivity.
- Next, use the command ifconfig to check the IP address of the connected APs.
- Use the command ssh [username]@[AP's IP address] to log into the AP's terminal interface. The default login credentials will be provided in the AP's manual or on the manufacturer's website.
- Once logged in, use the command iwconfig to check the wireless interface of the AP.
- Use the command ifconfig [interface] up to enable the wireless interface.
- Use the command iwconfig [interface] essid [SSID] to set the SSID of the wireless network.
- Use the command iwconfig [interface] key [password] to set the encryption key for the wireless network.
- Use the command dhclient [interface] to obtain an IP address for the AP.
- Use the command iptables --flush to flush the firewall rules.
- Use the command iptables -A INPUT -p tcp --dport 80 -j ACCEPT to allow incoming traffic on port 80.
- Use the command iptables -A INPUT -p tcp --dport 443 -j ACCEPT to allow incoming traffic on port 443.
- Use the command iptables -P INPUT DROP to block all other incoming traffic.
- Save the firewall rules by using the command iptables-save > /etc/iptables.rules
- Repeat steps 2 to 13 for additional APs.
- Now that all APs are up and running, you can assign them to specific areas or users within the network. For example, you can assign an AP to cover each floor of a building, or assign an AP to a specific department in a corporate environment.

- To assign an AP to a specific area or user, you can use the VLAN feature of your router or switch. You can create a VLAN for each area or user and assign the AP to the appropriate VLAN. You can use the command line interface of your router or switch to assign the AP to a specific VLAN.

The above specific steps and commands may vary depending on the make and model of the AP and the Linux-based operating system you're using. It is recommended to consult the AP's manual and the manufacturer's website for detailed instructions.

Managing Access to Specific Clients

Managing access to specific clients in a wireless network means controlling which wireless devices can connect to the network and which resources they can access. This is typically done by creating access control lists (ACLs) that define specific rules for different wireless clients based on their MAC addresses or IP addresses.

Example to Manage Access

Following is an example of how to manage access to specific clients on a Linux-based wireless access point (AP) using the hostapd software:

First, install the hostapd software by using the command apt-get install hostapd.

Next, create an access control list (ACL) file that defines the rules for different wireless clients. The file should list the MAC addresses of the wireless clients and the access level that should be granted to each client. For example:

```
00:11:22:33:44:55 1
00:11:22:33:44:56 2
```

Next, edit the hostapd configuration file located in /etc/hostapd/hostapd.conf and set the macaddr_acl option to 1 and the accept_mac_file option to the path of the ACL file created in step 2.

```
macaddr_acl=1
accept_mac_file=/etc/hostapd/acl.txt
```

Start the hostapd service by using the command systemctl start hostapd

Use the command iwconfig to check the wireless interface of the AP.

Use the command ifconfig [interface] up to enable the wireless interface.

Use the command iwconfig [interface] essid [SSID] to set the SSID of the wireless network.

Use the command iwconfig [interface] key [password] to set the encryption key for the wireless network.

Use the command dhclient [interface] to obtain an IP address for the AP.

Now, only the wireless clients that have their MAC addresses listed in the ACL file will be able to connect to the network and the access level of each client will be as defined in the ACL file.

Other Methods to Manage Access

In addition to the above steps, there are several other methods to manage access to specific clients on a wireless network.

One method is to use the built-in wireless controller feature of your router or switch. Many modern routers and switches come with wireless controllers that allow you to create and manage ACLs for wireless clients.

Another method is to use a wireless management software that can run on a Linux-based system. Some popular wireless management software for Linux include Network Manager and WICD. These software allows you to create and manage ACLs for wireless clients and also to monitor the performance of the wireless network.

It is also important to monitor the wireless network for any unauthorized clients that are trying to connect to the network. You can use tools such as Airodump-ng to capture wireless packets and identify any unauthorized clients.

In addition to the above, you may also want to consider using other security measures such as using WPA3 encryption and using a VPN to encrypt the data traffic.

Once you have set up the access control lists, you will want to monitor the network for any unauthorized clients that are trying to connect to the network. You can use tools such as Airodump-ng to capture wireless packets and identify any unauthorized clients.

It's recommended to run regular security checks on the wireless network and update the ACLs and security measures as necessary.

Configuring WPA Encryption

Overview

WPA (Wi-Fi Protected Access) is a security protocol for wireless networks that provides stronger security than the older WEP (Wired Equivalent Privacy) protocol. It uses a combination of the Advanced Encryption Standard (AES) algorithm and a Temporal Key Integrity Protocol (TKIP) to secure wireless communications.

Steps to Add WPA

Following is an example of how to add WPA encryption to a wireless network connection through the terminal on a Linux-based operating system, such as Ubuntu or Debian:

- First, use the command iwconfig to check the wireless interface of the wireless network card.
- Use the command ifconfig [interface] up to enable the wireless interface.
- Use the command iwconfig [interface] essid [SSID] to set the SSID of the wireless network.
- Use the command iwconfig [interface] key [password] to set the encryption key for the wireless network. Replace [password] with a strong and complex password.
- Use the command dhclient [interface] to obtain an IP address for the wireless network.
- Now, the wireless network is secured with WPA encryption and can only be accessed by devices that have the correct SSID and encryption key.

It's important to note that WPA2 is the successor of WPA and is more secure than WPA. Some systems may only support WPA2 encryption, so it's recommended to use WPA2 when possible.

In addition to the above steps, you may also want to consider using other security measures such as using WPA3 encryption and using a VPN to encrypt the data traffic. and also to keep in mind the security of the wireless network and update the security measures as necessary.

Configuring WPA2 Encryption

Overview

WPA2 (Wi-Fi Protected Access II) is a security protocol for wireless networks that provides stronger security than WPA. It uses the Advanced Encryption Standard (AES) algorithm to secure wireless communications. WPA2 also uses a Temporal Key Integrity Protocol (TKIP) or a Message Integrity Check (MIC) to ensure that the encryption keys are not compromised.

Steps to Add WPA2

Following is an example of how to add WPA2 encryption to a wireless network connection through the terminal on a Linux-based operating system, such as Ubuntu or Debian:

- First, use the command iwconfig to check the wireless interface of the wireless network card.
- Use the command ifconfig [interface] up to enable the wireless interface.
- Use the command iwconfig [interface] essid [SSID] to set the SSID of the wireless network.
- Use the command iwconfig [interface] key [password] to set the encryption key for the wireless network. Replace [password] with a strong and complex password.
- Use the command iwconfig [interface] key [password] enc [AES key] to set the AES encryption key for the wireless network. Replace [password] with a strong and complex password and [AES key] with the key generated by the network administrator.

- Use the command dhclient [interface] to obtain an IP address for the wireless network.
- Now, the wireless network is secured with WPA2 encryption and can only be accessed by devices that have the correct SSID and encryption key.

It's important to note that WPA2 is more secure than WPA and it's recommended to use WPA2 when possible.

Setting Up Firewalls

Functions of Firewalls

The term "firewall" refers to a type of network security system that monitors and controls network traffic coming into and going out of a network based on predetermined security rules and policies. The use of firewalls is essential for the protection of networks and devices against malicious software, unauthorized access, and other forms of online assault.

The most important function of a firewall is that it establishes a border between a guarded network and an external network. At this border, the firewall examines every data packet (a piece of information that can be transferred over the internet) that enters and exits the guarded network. With the assistance of a set of pre-configured rules, a firewall is able to differentiate between benign and malicious packets once the inspection process has been completed.

These packets are ignored by the firewall regardless of whether or not they are part of a rule set. This is done so that they do not enter the network that is being protected.

The content, as well as the source and destination of the information, are included in the information contained in this packet form. These may be different at each level of the network, as are the rule sets at each of those levels. These packets are analyzed by the firewalls, which then reformat them according to the rules that dictate where the protocol should send them.

Types of Firewalls

There are several types of firewalls, each with their own unique features and capabilities:

1. Network Firewalls: These firewalls are typically hardware-based and are placed at the perimeter of a network to control access to the network. They can be configured to allow or block specific types of traffic based on IP address, port number, and protocol. Examples of network firewalls include Cisco ASA and Juniper SRX.

2. Host-based Firewalls: These firewalls are typically software-based and are installed on individual devices such as laptops and servers. They can be configured to allow or block specific types of traffic based on IP address, port number, and protocol. Examples of host-based firewalls include Windows Firewall and iptables on Linux.

3. Application-based Firewalls: These firewalls are typically software-based and are designed to control access to specific applications and services. They can be configured to allow or block specific types of traffic based on the application or service being used. Examples of application-based firewalls include AppArmor and SELinux on Linux.

4. Next-Generation Firewalls (NGFW): These firewalls are a more advanced type of firewall that are designed to provide a deeper level of security by incorporating intrusion prevention, malware protection, and other advanced security features. Examples of NGFWs include Fortinet FortiGate and Check Point Next Generation.

Configuring Firewall using 'iptables'

Following is an example of how to configure a network firewall on Linux using the iptables firewall:

- First, install the iptables software by using the command apt-get install iptables
- Next, use the command iptables -A INPUT -p tcp --dport 22 -j ACCEPT to allow incoming SSH connections.
- Use the command iptables -A INPUT -p icmp -j ACCEPT to allow incoming ICMP connections.
- Use the command iptables -P INPUT DROP to drop all incoming connections not explicitly allowed.
- Use the command iptables-save > /etc/iptables.rules to save the firewall rules to a file.
- Use the command iptables-restore < /etc/iptables.rules to restore the firewall rules on reboot.

Monitoring Wireless Signal Strength

Wireless signal strength refers to the strength of the wireless signal that is being transmitted from the wireless access point (AP) to the wireless client device. This strength is measured in dBm (decibel-milliwatts) and is used to determine the quality and reliability of the wireless connection.

There are several factors that can affect wireless signal strength, including:

Distance: The farther a wireless client device is from the wireless AP, the weaker the wireless signal will be.

Obstacles: Walls, floors, and other physical obstacles can weaken or block wireless signals.

Interference: Other electronic devices such as microwaves, cordless phones, and Bluetooth devices can cause interference, which can weaken wireless signals.

Frequency: Different wireless frequencies such as 2.4GHz and 5GHz have different characteristics and can be affected differently by the above factors.

To monitor the wireless signal strength on a Linux-based operating system, you can use the command-line tool iwconfig. Following is an example of how to use iwconfig to check the wireless signal strength:

Open the terminal on your Linux system.

Use the command iwconfig to display information about the wireless interfaces on your system.

Look for the line that says "Link Quality" in the output. The value next to this line represents the signal strength in dBm. A higher number represents a stronger signal.

To check the signal strength of a specific interface, you can use the command iwconfig [interface]

To check the signal strength continuously, you can use the command watch -n 1 iwconfig [interface]

You can also use other tools such as wifi-strength, wicd-curses, and wavemon to monitor the wireless signal strength. These tools provide a graphical user interface (GUI) and more advanced features like historical logging and alerts.

Analyzing Wireless Network Traffic

Benefits of Network Traffic Analytics

Analyzing network traffic refers to the process of monitoring, capturing, and analyzing the data that is being transmitted over a network. This process is important for a variety of reasons, including:

- Identifying security threats: By analyzing network traffic, it is possible to identify potential security threats such as malware, hacking attempts, and other malicious activity.
- Troubleshooting network issues: Analyzing network traffic can help identify and resolve network problems such as slow performance, dropped connections, and other issues.
- Optimizing network performance: By understanding how the network is being used, it is possible to optimize network performance and ensure that the network is running at peak efficiency.
- Compliance: Analyzing network traffic can also be used to ensure compliance with regulatory and industry standards.

Popular Tools in Use

There are several tools that can be used to analyze network traffic, including:

- Wireshark: This is a popular open-source network protocol analyzer that can be used to capture and analyze network traffic.
- tcpdump: This is a command-line tool that can be used to capture and analyze network traffic.

- NetFlow Analyzer: This is a commercial tool that can be used to analyze network traffic and identify network problems.

- Nagios: This is a popular open-source monitoring tool that can be used to monitor network traffic and identify issues.

Using Wireshark for Network Analysis

Following is an example of how to use Wireshark to analyze network traffic on a Linux-based operating system:

- First, install Wireshark by using the command sudo apt-get install wireshark

- Launch Wireshark from the terminal by using the command wireshark

- Select the network interface that you want to capture traffic on.

- Click the "Start" button to begin capturing traffic.

- Once the capture is complete, you can use the various filters and analysis tools in Wireshark to analyze the captured traffic.

- You can filter the captured traffic by IP address, port number, and protocol, or by searching for specific keywords.

- You can also use the statistics and graphical tools in Wireshark to analyze the captured traffic in more detail.

Please keep in mind that this is just one of the many tools available to analyze the network traffic. The tool you choose will depend on your specific use case and the type of network traffic you need to analyze.

Updating Wireless Network Firmware

Understanding Network Firmware

Wireless network firmware refers to the software that is installed on wireless access points (APs) and other wireless networking devices. This firmware controls the basic functions of the device, such as wireless connectivity, security, and management.

Firmware updates and upgrades are important for several reasons, including:

- Security: Firmware updates often include security patches that can help protect against known vulnerabilities.
- Bug fixes: Firmware updates can also include bug fixes that can help improve the stability and performance of the device.
- New features: Firmware upgrades can add new features or capabilities to the device.

Updating and upgrading wireless network firmware can typically be done through the device's web-based management interface or via the command line interface (CLI) using Linux terminal. The process of updating and upgrading firmware varies depending on the device, manufacturer and the version of the firmware.

Steps to Upgrade Firmware

Following is a general example of how to upgrade firmware on a wireless access point (AP) using Linux terminal:

- Download the firmware upgrade file from the manufacturer's website.
- Connect to the wireless AP using SSH or Telnet.
- Use the command cd to navigate to the directory where the firmware upgrade file is located.
- Use the command mv [firmware file] /tmp to move the firmware file to the /tmp directory.
- Use the command sysupgrade -v /tmp/[firmware file] to upgrade the firmware on the wireless AP.

- Wait for the upgrade process to complete.

It is important to note that upgrading the firmware can be a sensitive task. Before upgrading, it is important to backup the current firmware and configurations, check compatibility, and test the new firmware on a non-production environment. It is also important to ensure that the device has enough power and that the upgrade process is done during a maintenance window to avoid disrupting the network.

Setting Up Virtual LAN

Understanding VLANs

A Virtual LAN (VLAN) is a logical grouping of network devices, regardless of their physical location. This allows for the segmentation of a LAN into smaller, more manageable groups, and enables the creation of separate broadcast domains within a single LAN.

VLANs are used to create multiple virtual networks on a single physical network, which can be useful for a number of applications, including:

- Security: VLANs can be used to create separate, secure networks for different groups of users or devices, such as guests, employees, or servers.

- Traffic management: VLANs can be used to segment network traffic and control the flow of data, allowing for better management of bandwidth and resources.

- Compliance: VLANs can be used to separate different types of traffic, such as voice and data, and to meet regulatory and industry standards.

There are several types of VLANs, including:

1. Port-based VLANs: This type of VLAN is created based on the physical ports of the switch. Devices connected to specific ports are placed in the same VLAN.

2. Tag-based VLANs: This type of VLAN is created based on the VLAN ID (tag) assigned to a frame. Devices with the same tag are placed in the same VLAN.

3. Protocol-based VLANs: This type of VLAN is created based on the Layer 3 protocol, such as IP or IPv6, used by the devices. Devices using the same protocol are placed in the same VLAN.

4. MAC-based VLANs: This type of VLAN is created based on the MAC address of the device. Devices with the same MAC address are placed in the same VLAN.

Setting Up Port-Based VLAN

Following is a general example of how to set up a port-based VLAN on a Linux-based operating system using the command-line tool vconfig:

- Install the vconfig package by using the command sudo apt-get install vconfig

- Use the command vconfig add [interface] [vlan_id] to create a new VLAN on the specified interface with the specified VLAN ID.

- Use the command ifconfig [interface].[vlan_id] to configure the IP address and other network settings for the new VLAN.

- Use the command vconfig set_name_type DEV_PLUS_VID_NO_PAD to set the VLAN name format.

- Use the command ifconfig [interface].[vlan_id] up to bring the VLAN up.

It is important to note that the VLAN setup and configuration will also depend on the type of switch and its capabilities. The switch's manual and website should be consulted for further instructions.

Hack#1: Best Practices on Wireless Networks

- Always use a strong encryption protocol such as WPA2 to protect your wireless network from unauthorized access.

- Change the default login credentials for your wireless router to prevent unauthorized access.
- Regularly update the firmware on your wireless router to ensure that any known vulnerabilities are patched.
- Use a firewall to protect your wireless network from incoming threats and to control the flow of traffic.
- Keep your wireless network's SSID hidden to prevent others from easily identifying and connecting to it.
- Disable remote management of your wireless router to prevent unauthorized access from outside your network.

Hack#2: Working Around Firewall Setup

- Keep your firewall rules updated and review them regularly to ensure that they are still relevant and effective.
- Use stateful firewalls that can track the state of a connection and only allow traffic that is part of an established connection.
- Use Access Control Lists (ACLs) to control access to specific resources.
- Use logging and monitoring tools to keep track of network activity and detect any suspicious activity.
- Use intrusion detection systems (IDS) and intrusion prevention systems (IPS) to detect and prevent malicious activity.

Hack#3: Use of Encryptions

- Use a VPN to encrypt your Internet traffic when accessing public Wi-Fi networks to prevent eavesdropping.
- Use HTTPS to encrypt the traffic between your browser and the websites you visit.
- Use SFTP or SCP instead of FTP to encrypt the traffic between your computer and the server.
- Use disk encryption software to encrypt the data on your hard drive in case your computer is lost or stolen.
- Use encrypted email services to secure the communication with your contacts.

www.ingramcontent.com/pod-product-compliance
Ingram Content Group UK Ltd.
Pitfield, Milton Keynes, MK11 3LW, UK
UKHW051353040826
14239UKWH00024B/346

9 788196 228514